Anyone for Cricket ?

NEIL WEBSTER.

Anyone for Cricket?

A Diary of an Australian Tour

BOB TAYLOR and DAVID GOWER
with the assistance of PATRICK MURPHY

PELHAM BOOKS
LONDON

First published by
Pelham Books Ltd
44 Bedford Square
London WC1
1979

ISBN 0 7207 1196 7

Photoset by DP Media Limited, Hitchin, Hertfordshire
and printed and bound in Great Britain by
Billing & Sons Limited, Guildford, London and Worcester

Contents

Guide to nicknames

God knows why, but all groups of sportsmen seem to have nicknames for each other. Some are bizarre, some are incomprehensible, some are cruel – one day a bright psychologist will write a learned treatise on just why professional sportsmen feel the need to use them. Till then we're happy to be part of the herd. Here's a guide to the names you'll see bandied about throughout the diary.

ARKLE   Derek Randall. Named after the racehorse because of his great speed in the field.

CHAT   Bob Taylor, because the other players insist he's the best at social functions.

CHILLY   Chris Old. C. Old, get it? Blame Willis for that one.

DUSTY, MILLS   Geoff Miller. Not much imagination there.

EMBERS, ERNIE   John Emburey. Ernie's his middle name.

FIERY, BOYCS, THATCH   Geoff Boycott, the first because he doesn't say too much and the last because of his transplanted hair.

GOOSE   Bob Willis, so named because whenever he can't think of the appropriate person's name, he calls them 'Goose'. A typical Willis sentence would be something like, 'Look, Goose, just put the goosey-goosey over there and it's fixed.'

GUY   Ian Botham. Short for Guy the Gorilla. A tribute to his strength and bravery as much as his liking for food. Also known as 'Both' or 'Tin Arse', the latter because in Pakistan last year he was always introduced by the locals as 'Iron Bottom'.

HENDO, SPIKE   Mike Hendrick. The first is obvious; the second comes from 'Spike Hendrome', a character mentioned in Hendo's 'Sam and Arthur' comedy routine with Geoff Miller.

HENRI   Phil Edmonds. His middle name.

JK   John Lever: Christian-name initials.

LULU   David Gower. Willis is responsible for that one, nobody's really sure why.

RAD   Clive Radley. A simple one.

SCAGG, BOZ, BREARS   Mike Brearley, the first because his parents come from Scagglesthorpe in Yorkshire, the second from his other nickname 'Scagglesthorpe Singh' which is foreshortened to Boz as in Boz Scaggs, the American singer.

TOLLY   Roger Tolchard.

ZAP, ZORRO   Graham Gooch who, with his dark looks and Mexican moustache, looks like Zapata, the Mexican revolutionary; also like Zorro.

Introduction

This is our account of the 1978/9 Australian tour as it happened;
we haven't had the benefit of hindsight to revise or varnish our
opinions, nor would we want to. Except for the final chapter,
when we assess the tour and its personalities, our diary is a faithful
record of our moods at that time. We felt it was worthwhile trying
to convey the pressures, the joys, the disappointments and the
distractions of representing our country on a four-month tour. We
realize the cricket fan normally judges a player by his performance out in the middle and we'd like that to remain the case – but
as sports fans ourselves, we always want to know more about our
favourite golfers, soccer stars or tennis players. This is an attempt
to let you understand more about a cricketer's life, rather than
how he plays the outswinger or makes a legside 'take' standing up.

Inevitably we'll write about the cricket, but we feel the expected
avalanche of books on the tour by the various cricket corre-
spondents will squeeze that particular fruit fairly dry. We're
indebted to Pat Murphy for editing our random thoughts and for
placing them in the context of the tour as it unfolded.

BOB TAYLOR and DAVID GOWER

1
Thoughts on the eve
of the tour

MURPHY Few doubted that the 1978/9 England touring party faced a tough test in Australia – and not just on the field. For the first time this century the ancient Ashes battle was threatened by a rival – World Series Cricket. Kerry Packer's brand of international cricket, although a failure in crowd terms in its first season, had creamed off some of the world's best players and made a serious bid for the attentions of many of Australia's cricket fans. As much would depend on England's ability to play attractive cricket against the young Australian side as on its potential to hold on to the Ashes. The neutral could well be forgiven for uttering a silent prayer that the series would be drawn three-all with the result of the sixth Test in doubt until the very last day on 16 February 1979.

England's tour party contained enough players to draw the crowds – batsmen like Gower, Randall and Gooch, an attacking all-rounder in Botham and a genuine fast bowler in Willis – but they were also a hard-headed, professional side well led by Mike Brearley. There were question marks, of course – Brearley's own form with the bat, the need for a resilient, well-organized batsman to come in at number 3, the doubts over the long-term fitness of Hendrick and Old and above all the mental attitude of Boycott. In just a few weeks before the start of the tour, this most complex and individual of Yorkshiremen had suffered a series of blows to his formidable pride – he had been passed over as England's vice-captain in favour of Willis, his mother had died and he had been sacked as Yorkshire's captain. For a time it seemed that these shattering events would prevent Boycott making the trip. But it was generally felt that his avowed determination to make hundreds of runs in Australia was the right one. Whether or not the intervening months would heal the breach between Boycott, some of his England colleagues and the new Yorkshire captain, Jack Hampshire, was another matter.

Another imponderable was the likely Australian line-up. Bob Simpson had retired after a successful holding operation against India and the West Indies and, with Jeff Thomson determined to rejoin Kerry Packer, the Australians were short of a penetrative opening bowler, experienced middle-order batsmen and a captain of proven Test-match expertise. The pressure on the young Australians was bound to be enormous: they would be facing an experienced, successful England team with the knowledge that a series of bad defeats would send many Australian cricket fans over to World Series Cricket.

Money would be a dominant feature on the tour. For the first time the England tourists had approached the question of sponsorship on a full-time basis. An agent had been appointed to handle promotional exercises on the tour and his work, added to generous prize money and tour fees, meant the England players would make far more than any other touring party to Australia – a fact that the cricket establishment was happy to emphasize in its continuing rivalry with the money- and ratings-conscious World Series Cricket.

For Bob Taylor and David Gower the trip presented an interesting contrast. This was to be Taylor's fourth tour of Australia – three with England and one with the Rest of the World – but for Gower it was his first senior England trip. Both players were highly regarded by fellow professionals and spectators alike: Taylor had now established himself as the world's number one wicket-keeper at the ripe old age of thirty-seven, while twenty-one year-old Gower had charmed many with his batting in the Test series against Pakistan and New Zealand. Doubts still existed about his ability to play long, major Test-match innings, but there was no disputing his quality or charisma. It was clear, in those final days before England left for Australia, that Gower and Taylor would be playing highly influential roles in the forthcoming series.

GOWER Things are so hectic in the last few days before we assemble at Lord's that it's taking some time to sink in. I'm not a very organized person and there are so many things to sort out that I'm grateful to my diary for keeping me straight. I share a flat with my Leicestershire colleague, Roger Tolchard. He's also been selected for the tour and the flat is in a fair old turmoil. There's packing to be done, TV and newspaper interviews to be finished, business matters to finalize and so many farewells to friends.

It sounds corny, I know, but the upsurge in my cricket career has happened so quickly. I think I'm still the same bloke – I go to the same pub, see the same faces, still live in the same place. I don't really want to change in personal terms. I don't want people to think, 'Look what's happened to him since he played for England.' It's been a great year so far and the cash rewards that flow from being a Test cricketer are tremendous, but I'd like to think David Gower's still the same person.

Once or twice last season it struck me that just five years ago I was still at school watching the Tests on the telly with the curtains closed and it seems unbelievable that I'm now a Test-match player. I never gave it serious thought in those days but it's been tremendous to play for England so soon after beginning my professional career. I've almost drifted into it. I *have* learned a lot in the last four years at Leicester – at some stage all the experienced players there have given me good advice and I've gone away to sort it all out for myself.

It was tremendous to do well in the Tests this summer, but I know this tour won't be easy because the Australians are notoriously hard to play against on their own ground. Having started so well with just a couple of failures when it didn't really matter, so many people expect me to succeed every time I bat for England, so my attitude, as well as my technique, has to be right. I realize I'll have to live with that kind of pressure because on paper our batting doesn't look as strong as our bowling. I'll be going out there to play my natural game, which includes the freedom to play shots, and I hope I can capitalize on whatever luck comes my way.

I'm still very much a junior player in the England side. I don't have to clean the boots or behave like a junior pro, but there is still a lot to learn from some very experienced players and I'll be keeping my eyes and ears open. People like Boycott, Brearley and Taylor were playing the game at top level when I was still at school, so there should be no shortage of people to turn to when things go wrong.

I get on fairly well with the media in Britain – it's all part and parcel of my career and they've been fair to me so far – but it will be interesting to see how the Aussie press treats us. They're supposed to be a lot more biased that the English press and we'll take a lot of anti-Pommie stick, I'm sure. Because we will be doing a lot of promotional work set up by the team's agent, I expect to be involved with a lot of press, TV and radio interviews and I'll try to do them as pleasantly as possible. We'll have to see how the official social functions go – the senior players tell me there's a lot of earbashing in store. We've got to carry the flag to a certain extent and I'm aware of the threat to established cricket from Kerry Packer, so I hope I can get through the various public-relations functions without too much soul-searching. The problem is that many people at functions don't realize that most cricketers would like to talk about other things when the day's play is over, unless it's about a technical matter that everyone in the conversation can understand.

I played in Perth a year ago and enjoyed it. I like the lifestyle out there: it's very casual. I think the sun tends to relax people and casual clothes suit me. I much prefer parties outdoors, which are a vast improvement on parties indoors. There *are* serious Australians, of course, but many of the ones I met last year felt as if they had to act out the Aussie image – the hard drinking, the swearing, treating their women roughly. But, funnily enough, when you get them on their own, talking calmly, they're okay. I'm sure I'll enjoy the social side of the tour.

I like reading – I got through about twenty-five books when I played in Perth last year – but I don't think I'll manage that this time. At Test level, you can't really focus your mind on serious reading at the end of the day's play. Mike Brearley can, but he's exceptional. So the evenings will be spent winding down with a few beers.

I love all types of music – Al Stewart, Neil Diamond, Genesis, Beethoven. I like harmonies and the technical side of a melody that'll stick in my mind. I admire the way musicians and composers can make a particular line of music stay in the brain for hours afterwards. So I hope I shan't lack relaxing music when I'm out there.

I'm pleased Roger Tolchard's coming on the tour. He's a good lad, who knows his cricket and has given me lots of good advice in the past – and I can always borrow money off him! He's not a bad squash player, either, although he maintains he only loses to me when he's been out late the night before. His batting could well be useful to England if some of the established batters don't succeed. Bob Taylor's a better keeper but I wouldn't be surprised to see Tolly play a Test or two as a batsman. He's done this before when Alan Knott kept wicket for England and Tolly made a vital 67 in India.

I think we've got a good side. I like Mike Brearley: he has the knack of getting a lot out of his team and is deservedly popular. He directs us well on the field, he's quick to go onto the attack and I never get the impression he's letting things slide. Bob Willis, the vice-captain, is another good lad. He seems to have gone from strength to strength in the last few years and his own brand of lewd humour should provide some lighter moments. He'll be a great asset when we're all feeling a bit down. Our pace bowling is one of our great strengths – there's Willis for speed, Botham for swing, Old and Hendrick for nagging accuracy and Lever for left-handed variation. Of the spinners, I expect Phil Edmonds to maintain his progress. Having established himself in the England team over the last year, he seems to have filled capably the gap left by Derek Underwood. It'll be interesting to see how much work Miller and Emburey get through because the Australian conditions don't normally favour off-spinners. The batsmen's main concern will be to make the most of the good wickets we're expecting. I must try to turn good starts into big innings. I've got to get through these sticky patches one often experiences during an innings – and carry on to a big score.

The Packer saga will be uppermost in a few minds. I've got no hard-and-fast thoughts on it – unlike some of the established England players in the party – but for me the best point about Packer is that he has woken up the administrators and made them pay us something nearer our true worth. That was indirectly due to Packer, though it doesn't mean I approve of the principle of World Series Cricket. By taking established players away from Test cricket, WSC has given people like me a chance to get into it – but I accept that this is a selfish way of looking at it.

We'll just have to see how the two forms of cricket co-exist in the next few months and whether there's a chance of a compromise. But many of our England side are strongly anti-Packer and there'll have to be a lot of hard bargaining if there's to be a solution.

It seems as if the domestic season ended only yesterday, yet here we are, at the end of October, flying away to Australia. It can be a hard grind sometimes, but the prospect's exciting. It's a big country, the social side of life out there suits me, I've got some very sociable companions in the tour party and I'm getting well paid to play for my country. Can't be bad, can it?

TAYLOR   This will be the first time I've been to Australia as England's number one, and even though that's stemmed from Alan Knott signing for Packer, it's still a marvellous feeling nobody can take from me. I always thought Alan a great keeper and a great bloke, and I can understand why his superior batting always got him the nod over me – but I'd be less than human if I didn't get restless as permanent reserve on all those tours.

It used to be worse in Australia. At the innumerable social functions we had to attend, people would sometimes come up to me, look at my lapel badge and say, 'R. W. Taylor – who are you?' That would really hurt; there I was, one of my country's sixteen best cricketers, and yet some people wouldn't know me. I hope I won't have to explain who I am to many on this tour. I like to think I've taken the chance Knotty's departure has given me and I've been satisfied with my form since I took over in Pakistan a year ago. I also think my batting's underrated – I can't change the course of a Test with brilliant strokeplay *à la* Knott – but I'm often able to keep an end up for a few hours while a better strokemaker blazes away at the other end. I'll try to do that as much as possible in this Ashes series, because we all know the England batting isn't terribly strong.

I like touring, although my wife, Cathy, normally has to push me on the plane when the departure day arrives. I'm very much a homebird, always have been. I live in a lovely part of Staffordshire near where I was born. Cathy and I have been married for seventeen years, and I've got two lovely kids. Cathy's not the kind of cricketer's wife who sticks her oar in, she's calm and understanding and she's been a tremendous help to my career. At the end of a day's play, I love to lock the door, forget about cricket and be with my family. I'll miss them very much this tour and will have my favourite photo of the four of us at my bedside whichever hotel I'm in. I'll have to throw myself into my cricket and the various off-field responsibilites and look forward to 19 January when Cathy joins me for the last month of the tour.

I think our social responsibilities will be very important on this trip. I'm very conscious that I'm representing the traditional side of cricket – a game that's been very good to me – and our side will have to be good ambassadors for our country. The threat of Packer is a real one – although I wouldn't entertain playing his brand of instant, gimmicky cricket even if he paid me fifty grand a year – and our tour party must get out and meet people in Australia, talk about the advantage of traditional Test cricket, and play the kind of stuff that will get the crowds pouring in. I think we'll get the Australian public on our side because basically there's nothing like England v. Australia; they love to thrash the Poms. It'll be terrific playing in front of 70,000 at Melbourne, something that surely Packer cricket can't approach because it doesn't have this national identification. I'm sure a lot of Packer players know this and I can't believe that players like Derek Underwood are happier playing forty-over matches on park pitches than representing England in a Test match.

We'll all be watching the Packer situation closely in the next few months – not least of all because next season's World Cup in England is threatened unless there's a compromise soon. Last April at the Cricketers' Association AGM, England players like myself, Ian Botham, Mike Hendrick and John Lever outlined firm proposals to ban games in England against teams containing Packer players. We were persuaded to leave those proposals on the table pending discussions involving the Association, World Series Cricket and the cricket authorities. I fervently hope there'll be some sort of compromise worked out, but I'm a bit cynical about Packer's real intentions when he continues to sign up all these players – in the last month, the Pakistanis Miandad, Haroon and Sarfraz and the Australian Jeff Thomson. I was one of the England side at Karachi earlier this year that refused to play against Pakistan if they selected their Packer players. I know that those players feel even stronger now about such an issue and unless something is sorted out soon the England players won't take part in next summer's World Cup matches if the other countries select Packer men. I feel that these blokes can't have their cake and eat it – they were happy to learn their trade with established cricket and become international stars, and then turned their backs on it when someone came along with more money.

Mind you, Packer has helped us all earn more money – although I'm not sure if that was his original intention. It's time cricket was put on a proper wage-earning level and, thanks to the Cornhill International sponsorship, that is happening. For me, it's all come right just when I wanted it – I'm thirty-seven, feel very fit, I'm my country's top keeper and I'm being handsomely paid for the privilege. So thanks for your help, Mr Packer.

Wicket-keepers *do* mature with age and I honestly think I can keep going for another five years. I've never put on any weight since I started playing for Derbyshire nearly twenty years ago, and having played semi-professional football for Port Vale, I think I know the value of fitness. I don't drink a lot – maybe a pint and a gin and tonic – I watch the calories, always try to get a lot of sleep and as a result I always feel like playing cricket. I've got one big personal aim – I'd like to top John Murray's all-time record of keeper's dismissals. I'm about two hundred behind and if I keep going for another five years I should do it. I hope that doesn't sound conceited – it's just that all professional sportsmen should have personal goals, otherwise they're not stretching themselves. I'll never be complacent about my job and if I can set a new record for the kind of established cricket I respect, I'll be a proud man. It will be my way of showing my gratitude to traditional cricket.

Knowing the Aussie conditions, I'm hoping for an easier time behind the stumps than in Pakistan last winter. Over there, the ball keeps very low and sometimes I even had to stand up to people like John Lever and Ian Botham. But in Australia the ball comes through truer – although there's a fair degree of bounce – and the air is thinner, so that the ball will come quickly through. So I'll have to sharpen up my reactions every day before I keep wicket, otherwise I might end up snatching at the ball when it's almost past me.

I hope we fare better than the last England team in Australia. Four years ago, Mike Denness had all the bad luck that was going but we still weren't in the same class as the Aussies. They caught everything, they batted better and we ended up shell-shocked by Lillee, Thomson and Walker. It wasn't a particularly happy tour off the field either – some of the players were distracted by their wives and children, others didn't give a hundred per cent to the captain and some retired into their shells. I don't think there's much danger of that this time – Mike Brearley has the respect of us all, Bob Willis is a tremendous character and a popular choice as vice-captain and the decision to have two men, Ken Barrington and Doug Insole, as managers is a wise one. They both know the game inside out; Kenny's the great enthusiast who still wishes he was playing, while Doug is quieter, very shrewd and, because he was chairman of the Test and County Cricket Board when the Packer storm broke last year, he'll be vital when negotiations with World Series Cricket begin.

Much will depend on Geoff Boycott and how he reacts to being passed over as vice-captain. In Pakistan and New Zealand he wasn't in my view a great success when he took over as skipper from the injured Mike Brearley and the responsibility clearly affected his batting. He's very much a loner but we all respect his batting ability – although I feel he doesn't dictate enough to the bowlers – and I hope he'll swallow his pride and score hundreds of runs for us. An England side with Boycott is always that much harder to beat and the Aussies know that well enough.

I hope we don't have to rely too much on Bob Willis for the early breakthrough. He's a great trier and a superb Test-match performer, but he's done so well in the last couple of years that there's a danger to overbowl him. I've known Bob since we roomed together on Ray Illingworth's tour of Australia in 1970/71 and I've always admired his guts and his contribution to team spirit off the field. Mike Brearley's very good in human relations and I'm sure he will realize that Bob must be deployed sparingly in the State games and only used on full throttle in the Tests. He looks like being the only genuine fast bowler on either side and we must nurture that asset.

All of us have things to prove – David Gower must show that his attractive strokeplay this summer wasn't a flash in the pan. He has to learn to battle through the stodgy periods when he can't get the ball away, he must get over his square cuts to avoid being caught in the gully and he must cure the habit of chipping the ball over mid-on, instead of going through with the shot. His natural talent is immense and I feel sure he's intelligent enough to come through as a major Test batsman. But he'll get a few rollickings before the tour's over – and they'll be good for him.

My Derbyshire team-mate Geoff Miller must conquer his self-doubts. He's a fine all-rounder but he takes too much notice of the critics who say he still hasn't scored a maiden hundred and that he bowls his off-spinners too flat. He *does* lack a bit in flight variation, unlike Derek Underwood whose greatness lay in his ability to vary the pace and flight according to whether it was a Test match, a county game or a one-day slog – but I've kept to Mills for several seasons now and I rate him. He's still very young but already he's done valuable things for England and I hope he'll bat with more conviction and give the ball a bit more air at certain key moments.

Phil Edmonds must learn to concentrate – sometimes he seems in a world of his own. Of course, he's intelligent (Cambridge degree and all that) but for someone with such tremendous natural talent he's taken a long time to blossom. With his batting ability he should be an accepted all-rounder by now. He and Mike

Brearley – men of similar intellect – often have a few words and it will be interesting to see how Mike handles Phil.

Mike Hendrick and Chris Old must rid themselves of this injury-prone tag and show the kind of consistency to match their top-class bowling skills – and it's time Chris started getting the runs his batting warrants. Derek Randall must show whether his spell in county cricket away from the Test area has tightened up his technique. It'll be interesting to see if Clive Radley – a late-comer, like myself, to Test cricket – can capitalize on his fine start against Pakistan and New Zealand. He's got the temperament and it'll be fascinating to see how he improvises when the Aussies cut off his favourite mid-wicket area.

We've all got our own targets and some of us will fail. Cricket can be a cruel game sometimes and it's also a selfish one – yet, more often than not, if you are selfish and succeed, it benefits the team. The balance must be struck between doing a job for the team and just pleasing oneself. It'll be interesting to see how many of us strike that balance. We're lucky – we have a good captain, a first-class managerial back-up, and a happy, settled side. I wonder how we'll be described in four months' time?

2
Early days

GOWER Departure day. Starts at 9.40 when a local TV station arrives for a final interview – I'm still in the bath. We set off late for London with myself and Tolly, my girlfriend Vic and another friend. Drop Vic at Paddington, neither of us wants a long time to say goodbye and by the time we arrive at Lord's things are happening fast enough to subdue the emotions. Organized chaos reigns. Plane departs near enough on time by air standards, sign a few autograph sheets and then doze off. Give Bahrain Airport a miss, take a stroll in Singapore, try the film on the plane but can't keep eyes open.

TAYLOR Got to Lord's at midday, just like a bring-and-buy sale at the Indoor School where we picked up all our free presentations; clothes, equipment and god knows what else – after-shaves, deodorants, games, golf balls, you name it. Photographers engaged by firms for whom we were doing advertising or promotions kept clicking away – the main one, Perkins Engines, had the team gathered around a huge diesel engine and when the photographer said, 'Smile,' Mike Hendrick said, 'I can't, it's on my toe!' Reception given by Cornhill and then fly out at 9.45 pm by Qantas – a deal's been done with the TCCB for cheap travel and in return we'll be giving free coaching sessions in the Test-match centres. On board I meet Bill Jacobs, who managed the Rest of the World side in Australia six years ago when I played under Gary Sobers. Bill was coming back from Ireland with an Australian Rules football team, comparing hurling with the Aussie national game. Good flight, enjoyed the film, starring Peter Falk as a comic detective.

October 26

GOWER Arrive fairly smoothly at Sydney Airport. Run into the expected battery of cameramen. Feel okay, the press are already at the hotel in Adelaide. Give the first interview – to Mike Coward from the local *Advertiser*. Nod off at 5 pm, team meeting at 6, succumb to sleep at 10. My first room-mate is Chris Old; he knows what's going on, he's had his share of tours. He's got his cassettes organized for our room already. Boycott shows a touch of experience by getting himself a car, instead of the ones we get by courtesy from Avis cars and Chrysler.

Got time to think about batting – Willis bowls me some bouncers in the nets, I hit one, nick one, and duck a couple more. I'm trying to discipline myself to playing on bouncy wickets, to organize the brain to leave the bouncers alone.

Still feeling the effects of the flight, though not as much as last year's to Perth. Not giving things too much of a crack yet. Early training session . . . four laps of the pitch – bloody awful.

TAYLOR Jet lag made me miscalculate the time when a schoolboy hopped onto our bus and asked for autographs; I asked him why he wasn't at school, he said he didn't have to be there till 9 o'clock, I looked at my watch and it said 10.55! Met by Sir Donald Bradman when we finally arrived at Adelaide – amazing how he manages to remember everyone's christian names, and can hold a personal conversation with every player. An impressive man.

Most players went straight to bed when we got to the hotel but I didn't want to sleep mid-afternoon and went for a stroll with Doug Insole and Bernie Thomas. Next day all the lads who went to bed in the afternoon told me they woke up in the early hours of the morning and couldn't get back to sleep. Bob Willis had his own remedy for that – he went for a five-mile run in the park at 4 am!

Enjoyed the first training session, everyone in good shape considering the jet lag. Several laps of the Adelaide Oval and a good fielding session. In the afternoon, batting practice, but thank goodness not compulsory – the nets were very green and damp owing to the recent bad weather and the ball moved all over the place, ideal conditions for Hendo and Chilly.

In the evening, Chilly, Lulu and myself invited by an old friend,

Harry Kershaw, for roast beef and Yorkshire pudding and tatties. Made me think about home, but an enjoyable evening, talking over past tours and good times together.

MURPHY   The team made an impressive start in the public-relations stakes. Mike Brearley said the right things at the press conferences, striking a balance between an awareness of his team's strengths and a realization that the Australians always manage to find some unknown players who in a few months are established Test cricketers. Brearley said he expected to bat at number five, he thought Gooch and Boycott would make an ideal opening pair. He told the press that Gower was one of the best timers of the ball he'd ever seen, that Taylor was a great wicket-keeper and poured scorn on the rumour that an injury to Ian Botham's left wrist just before the tour started would keep him out of action for more than the expected fortnight. Brearley himself admitted he'd finally abandoned the exaggerated backlift he'd been using for the last couple of seasons at the crease. He'd changed to a more orthodox, crouched stance with a reduced backlift in an attempt to improve on a Test batting average of just 25 with a top score of 91. Assistant manager Barrington – cheerfully bowling his leg-spinners in the nets for hours at the age of forty-seven – pronounced himself delighted with the England team's attitude: 'This is the fittest bunch of lads I've toured with. And I'm staggered by the high standard of catching since we arrived, they've adjusted so well to the bright light and the speed of the ball through the air.' Barrington's optimism over England's quality in the field proved to be fully justified.

The London bookmakers, perhaps reflecting excessive patriotism rather than an awareness of the famous Australian resilience, made England the strongest favourites ever to tour Australia. They were quoted at 8/1 to win the series, with the home side 11/4 and 3/1 for a drawn series.

As expected, the spectre of Kerry Packer loomed large and early. The Australian papers were full of Packer's plans to take his teams to the West Indies, of his huge financial outlay on night cricket, of his offer to pay the parking-meter fees of all the spectators who attended his matches in Sydney and of Jeff Thomson's High Court action to free himself from the Australian Board of Control and rejoin Packer.

October 28

GOWER Team photos in our 'admiral's gear', our nickname for the official tour outfit. More laps, stretches and nets in the morning and afternoon. Watch cricket and golf on the box and go to a trotting meeting in the evening. The whole side there, apart from Boycs and Guy. My card is marked for me, so I do quite well – ten of us put a hundred dollars on number 4 in the 4th and it skates home.

TAYLOR I picked up a few dollars at the trotting meeting, but not the expected free meal. Ken Barrington arranged the night out and told us there'd be a free meal thrown in so we wouldn't have to spend our daily £6.50 meal allowance. Not so – and Kenny got some stick.

October 29

GOWER Phone call soon after my eyes open. It's from Vic. Lovely way to wake up and I find it very difficult to put the phone down. Write my first letter home – to Vic. More training and nets, pose for photos for local paper. Quiet grog with Chilly, Chat and Gooch and early night. Still restless.

October 30

More training and nets. We get there late because we wait for Boycott, so Bernie Thomas awards us extra bleedin' laps. Nets boring as ever – I really want to get in the middle and have a crack. First major earbashing of the tour at the Lord Mayor of Adelaide's reception. Goes smoothly, mainly due to beer and the presence of a couple of South Australia players. Back at the motel Chilly and I have a small party in our room and the meal allowance disappears on wine! Instantaneous sleep occurs on pillow contact.

TAYLOR Bob Willis invited all those interested to a barbecue at a friend's house outside Adelaide – another free meal! Excellent food and hospitality. Weather still cool, so we ate indoors and initially all the players sat together while the other guests were across the other side. But when the food arrived things became more relaxed and we had a great laugh with a character called Leo the Lion – so called because, although raised in Australia, he was born in Britain and remains a great patriot, loves the royalty and comes out with some marvellous Alf Garnett style remarks. A very likeable chap, he stood there, thrilled to be in the company of the England cricket team while his Aussie friends pulled his leg goodnaturedly.

More good news on the food front. I met a wholesale oyster dealer who let me have fifteen dozen rock oysters – five of us, Chilly, Goose, JK, Ken Barrington and myself, ate the lot in one session – beautiful!

November 1
First game, the South Australian Country XI at Renmark, 120 miles north-east of Adelaide. Fly into Renmark at 10.15 am, there's no proper runway, it's just a field. We get a very nice reception with a party of schoolchildren waving and cheering themselves hoarse when we get off the plane. A major fruit-growing area, there's plenty of fresh fruit, including some delicious fresh orange juice. A well-organized match, marvellous hospitality and we're all given a nice memento of our visit – an original miniature painting of an Australian scene. The game's drawn and the irony is that I'm twelfth man – after three tours of Australia as reserve keeper, I'm still taking out the drinks! Everyone a little bit scared of the return trip, flares are lit by the locals, and, added to a blaze of car lights, we manage to take off without the pilot hitting any kangaroos! A good flight back to end a most enjoyable day.

GOWER About 4,000 turned up to watch us, but it was fairly tame and an average game. I had trouble in working myself up to full concentration. Fairly happy with my form, but still want to play in the first State game before making any serious judgements. Bob Minns, the Oxford and Kent batsman of the early 1960s (also from my old school), lives in the area and he's now a wine expert. He presents Brears with a case of wine.

MURPHY   The Renmark trip was generally judged a great success. The players got some much-needed practice and as many spectators came to see the game as can be expected for England's matches against the State sides. Traditional cricket has a strong hold in the area – a point confirmed last year when the West Indies played the Rest of the World in a Packer match not far away up the Murray River. Most spectators left in disgust because of the exhibition nature of the match. The fact that England played against the local cricketers added greatly to the day's enjoyment for the spectators. At the start of a tour where public relations was going to play an important part, it was a valuable day.

Gower played a few characteristic shots before dragging a wide ball onto his stumps for 26. The best innings came from Radley who timed the ball perfectly for his 64 in 94 minutes. The England fielding looked sharp.

One shadow hung over the day – the news that Geoff Boycott was having trouble with his knee. Physiotherapist Bernard Thomas diagnosed it as bursitis and Boycott said his left knee was hurting every time he played forward – quite a dilemma for a right-handed batsman. He thought the problem had been caused by too much practising in the first week of the tour. Certainly England were watching the medical bulletins on Boycott's knee with uncommon interest because a fit Boycott was an essential part of the tour strategy. As it turned out, Boycott's influence on the series proved surprisingly insubstantial.

November 2

GOWER   A rest day. I'm playing tomorrow in the opening match against South Australia, so I rest up at the poolside with JK, Brears, Rad, and Doug Insole. Write a letter to my mother, although I struggle to think of news to give her. After lunch Rad, Arkle and I borrow Boycott's car and test out the beach – not as impressive as Perth but it *is* only early summer. A Benson and Hedges reception in the evening.

TAYLOR   Eight of us played golf on a beautiful course. Chilly and I ended up playing with a middle-aged Irishman named Michael

Byrne who'd been over here since 1946. After a few holes Guy joined us for some exercise because his wrist injury means he still can't practise much. As usual Guy didn't spare the swear words as we played the course. While I was walking down the fairway I asked Mr Byrne what he did for a living – he answered, 'I'm a Roman Catholic Priest.' I was very embarrassed and apologized for Guy's language, but Father Byrne grinned and said, 'That's alright, Bob, it was old stuff anyway. I'm still waiting to hear something different.'

November 3

Our first State game. We lose the toss and field all day. It's very hot – about eighty degrees – but we all stuck to the task and the bowlers worked hard. A good day for me – five victims, including a stumping. They finish on 281 for 9. One of their openers, Rick Darling, has played for Australia and is strongly fancied to play in the Tests but Goose sorted him out. He's a compulsive hooker and Goose fed him with bouncers until he hooked one straight down square-leg's throat. We shan't forget Darling and the hook shot if he plays in the Tests. Everyone shattered at close of play – I fell asleep in the bath back at the hotel!

November 4

GOWER   I get to bat, play like a . . . but left-hander's luck sees me through to 73. Rodney Hogg pins Rad, he needs seven stitches in his head and he's also out hit-wicket. Not too encouraging for me to take guard on the blood. Fairly happy at the end of the day, got a couple of bruises but dare say they won't be the last. In the evening went out to a Cornhill Insurance man's house with Chat, Chilly and JK – place full of babies but as the beer and the evening progressed, things relaxed – perhaps because the choice of music was left to me! Very pleasant evening.

TAYLOR   Hogg looked very quick and bouncy and is a definite Test candidate – but I've got doubts over his stamina. He suffers from asthma and can only bowl short spells. When I bat, I'm given out caught off my toe at slip – I'm very disgusted. When South Australia bat again, I get three more victims (including another stumping), eight dismissals in the match, a pleasing start for me. Edmonds bowls well to take 5 for 52 in 23 eight-ball overs.

November 6

GOWER　We throw the game away. We only needed 229 to win and I was 43 not out overnight with the total 89 for 3. But as soon as I got my fifty I was out to a poor stroke (caught at slip driving at a wide one) and the rot set in. Brears ran himself out and only Chilly and JK with some long handle gave our scoreline any respectability. I batted much better than in the first innings but annoyed at my dismissal. Drinks with the opposition after the game – they're delighted and who can blame them? However I don't think our defeat was all that significant, even if it was the first time an England touring side had lost to South Australia since 1925.

TAYLOR　We didn't bat well and our middle-order batting crumbled to the medium pacers in both innings. But we've learned a lot from this match, not least about the problems of acclimatization and that we'll need to work hard to beat these Aussies. They play it hard and relentlessly and this will shake us up at the right time. Our team spirit is still very good and Mike Brearley's not the kind of bloke to panic.

MURPHY　It was only South Australia's second win in two years and although the England camp played it down, there were some disturbing signs. Radley's injury meant he would need some time to recover his nerve and timing before he could go in first wicket down – so his place in the First Test in just over three weeks' time was very much in jeopardy. Boycott – although dismissed by Hogg twice in sixteen balls – looked the only batsman capable of building a long innings. Already pressure was being put on Brearley to open with Boycott and it looked as if England's chronic batting problems weren't over. There were some consolations though – Gower played some lovely shots, Edmonds and Miller bowled their spinners well and all the bowlers got through some hard work. Taylor kept wicket immaculately, giving away just two byes in a combined total of 460 and his first-innings stumping of Langley was loudly applauded by the crowd.

Taylor's opinions on Hogg are an example of how even professional, experienced cricketers can misjudge a player. Hogg turned out to be Australia's most penetrating bowler – his stamina was never a problem and he was consistently fast and accurate. Boycott's sore knee continued to trouble him. His complaint was understood to be an inflamed tendon – rather more serious than the originally diagnosed housemaid's knee – and he was now needing three daily sessions of electrotherapy treatment. But Botham continued to make good progress with his wrist injury and expected to be playing in ten days' time.

Meanwhile in Sydney, Jeff Thomson's bid to play for Kerry Packer this season suffered a setback when a High Court judge ruled that he cannot play for World Series Cricket until April. Thomson, who says he'll never appear for the official Australian side again, was said to be bound by his contract with the Australian Board of Control. Thomson said later that he'd still like to play for Queensland against England 'so I can have a crack at Geoff Boycott'. Thomson's optimism proved unfounded – he had to kick his heels until WSC went to the West Indies in March.

November 7

TAYLOR   Melbourne. Staying at the Hilton Hotel. Meet Johnnie Miller, Hale Irwin and Nick Faldo, who're staying there while playing in the Australian Open. Interesting chat, I'm fascinated by the mental demands of golf and the fact that you can never think you've mastered that game. When I retire from county cricket I shan't play it again – not even locally – and I can see myself getting bitten by the golf bug.

Terrible weather. The heavy rain makes net practice impossible, have to train in the gym. Back to the hotel where the atmosphere's very light-hearted. It's Melbourne Gold Cup day, the big event in the horse-racing calendar and the hotel's swamped with partygoers – champagne cocktails all over the place. Outside it's almost like a religious holiday with bars and restaurants closed – the Aussies like their racing. The team have a sweep on the race, I draw a good one – called Panamint, trained by the millionaire Australian Robert Sangster and ridden by a top jockey called Higgins. Doesn't win, but I also have a dollar and a half bet on the tote on the eventual winner so I don't do badly, picking up about fifteen dollars. Guy wins the team sweep and he also puts a side bet on the winner – lucky blighter!

GOWER   After training, squash with Zap until noon. Repair to join Chilly in the pub who's having trouble sleeping and partakes of a liquid lunch to try to kip in the afternoon – could be a good theory. Then some pool and table tennis and Hendo, Zap and I try the sauna at the Hilton. Supposed to be mixed but no luck today. I pick up 20 dollars in the team sweep for the third-placed horse in the Gold Cup. Everything dominated by the race, the hotel awash with champagne. There's even a champagne breakfast but sadly by that time I was in no state to join.

November 8

TAYLOR   A game against a Victoria Country XI at Leongatha, 85 miles south-east of Melbourne, a big farming area. Because of heavy rain, conditions aren't good but we agreed to play because it would be a shame to disappoint the locals – it's not every year Test players come to their town. The wicket is dreadful, one up, one down – I play forward to a good-length ball which shot along the ground and badly bruised my toe. The next ball lifted, hit me on the glove and split the leather. We scraped together 130 and then bowled them out for 59 – a good game! Food and hospitality very good in the nearby golf club after the match.

GOWER   Some very pleasant scenery on the way to Leongatha, although that's not the idea of coming 12,000 miles. Fair-sized crowd (4,000) considering the population of Leongatha is 3,659. Bloody awful game but the locals are overjoyed at the proceedings. Can't say I share their feelings, although as long as they're happy, then we've done some good PR work. On the coach trip back, Dusty and Hendo give us their Sam and Arthur routine – impressions of the regulars in a Derbyshire tap room. Very good value. The press get stuck into the tins of Foster's Lager just for a change.

November 9

TAYLOR   No chance of net practice again because the wickets are too damp, getting rather frustrating. Where are all these blue Aussie skies? Some light relief when we had to do a commercial in the dressing room for the Milk Marketing Board – all the team holding glasses of milk. Things slowed down somewhat by our lads' sense of humour – their versions of the 'takes' rather different to those of the director. Eventually we were sick of the sight of milk! Then another official do – a cocktail reception thrown by the Victoria Cricket Association. The Prime Minister Malcolm Fraser appeared briefly before going on to the Lord Mayor's banquet. As he was leaving he told the assembly that he wished he could stay – afterwards a cynical local told me that was the best speech he's ever heard the PM make.

November 10

Start of the game against Victoria. We are introduced to the PM beforehand and the usual booing for a politician breaks out. Those of us not playing – Boycott, Willis, Miller, Botham and myself – help out coaching some kids. It's organized by Frank Tyson, the former England fast bowler and now Victoria's coach. In the evening, Scagg, Hendo and myself are invited to dinner by Peter Mountford the former Oxford University pace bowler who now teaches over here. A couple of other schoolmasters and their wives join us and after a while one of the ladies starts being caustic about the way Hendo and I talk. She said sarcastically she couldn't understand Northerners – if I hadn't been enjoying a friend's hospitality I would have told her a few things. There are times when an England tourist really has to count to ten.

GOWER   The damp conditions lead to a slow wicket for the Victoria match which means a slow game, which equals boredom. You had to loft the ball to get any runs on such a sodden outfield and it all must have been hard going for the spectators. Henri and Embers bowl well to get Victoria out for 254 and I'm pleased with running out Laughlin with a quick underarm throw from cover – my second in a week. The batsman who takes no risks is in little danger and Brears grinds to 76 not out in four and a half hours.

Arkle plays well but he and I sacrifice our wickets to Wiener, a fairly average off-spinner. Their bowlers aren't bad, though – Hurst and Callen were lively opening bowlers even though the wicket blunted their effectiveness. The leg-spinner Jim Higgs looked the most likely to strike without actually doing so.

In the evening Chilly, JK, Rad, Guy, Henri and myself settle down for a chat in the team rest room and after Chilly goes to bed the rest of us nip up the road to a party, bearing a couple of bottles of wine each. It's going strong when we get there but unbelievably there are groups of men and females not talking to each other. Everything's very genial but most people want to talk cricket. Easy way out of that – talk to the women, they don't understand it!

November 11

TAYLOR   In the evening six of us go to a trotting meeting. We're wined and dined in the VIP lounge and looked after excellently. I have a bet called a 'trifecta', which means three horses at a six-dollar stake and you must get them in the frame in no particular order. I lost in the first seven races but came up trumps in the last one and so broke even on the night.

The next day's play is called off because of rain, so we train indoors, play squash and after lunch some of us go to the hotel sauna. I go in first with a towel round my waist (it's mixed), the door opens and . . . sorry to disappoint, a fella walks out. He asks me if I'm going to use the sauna, I confirm this and he tells me his Excellency the Governor General of Australia is inside with his bodyguards. I said I didn't mind sharing because I had no weapons to hide. We were all introduced and he seemed a very nice man.

November 12

GOWER   This rain's getting me down, it's really adding to our experience of wet-weather cricket. You just don't expect to encounter this in Australia. Pretty miserable day after last night's party, have to prop the matchsticks into the eyes. Everything's dead in Melbourne on a Sunday, even the hotel bars are closed, so the Hilton's devoid of its usual crowd of socialites. Play Zap at squash again and shoot a fair bit of pool.

It rains again overnight and we don't start the game until 2 pm. Pointless exercise – Brears gets his hundred and the rest of us get bored. Pleased for Brears, though – should help his confidence. We even have to field for fifty minutes at the end as the game peters out into a draw. Later on a meal and a couple of beers with an old school colleague. Then a late-night visit from three very boring and gruesome young ladies. It took some time to persuade them there was no future in Room 1008 and they were ejected. Just because we're 12,000 miles from home doesn't mean there's any need to lower one's standards.

November 14

TAYLOR   Off to Canberra where we go to two receptions in one evening – first the Governor General's, then to the British High Commissioner. When I met up again with the Governor General I told him I nearly didn't recognize him with his clothes on. Later on his wife and daughter had a good laugh with me about the sauna incident. All in all a very enjoyable evening at both receptions.

GOWER   I enjoyed the High Commissioner's reception more because Chilly, Henri and I sat round a table with three ladies of varying ages whose brains are tested by Henri's deliberately outspoken views on life. Interesting to check their reactions when he comes out with an outlandish theory. I chip in from time to time, trying to avoid things getting too serious and time and wine disappear quite freely.

A petrol strike's on the cards – no doubt it's been blamed on those bloody Pommie trade unionists.

MURPHY   The events of the last week hadn't exactly helped England's Test-match preparations. Both matches had given little opportunity for batting practice and the conditions hadn't done much for the bowlers either. The wickets weren't like the usual Australian ones – these had little pace or bounce and took spin. On the credit side, Randall looked in good shape. His half-century against Victoria was full of elegant shots and daring improvisations. With Radley still struggling after his blow on the head against South Australia, an in-form Randall was an integral part of England's Test line-up and he helped compensate for Boycott's decline. The tour party was pleased to see Brearley reach his first hundred in first-class cricket since July 1977, even if it was an unmemorable effort. His success and Gooch's continued. Unlucky failures were bound to mean more pressure on the captain to open with Boycott, a pressure he eventually acknowledged.

The England players had a good look at Hurst and Higgs, two bowlers likely to be playing in the Tests. Hurst looked genuinely quick for a few overs and Higgs impressed in a long bowl of 39 overs. He bowled a good top-spinner, didn't try the googly but remained accurate. It was difficult to understand why Graham Yallop, Victoria's captain (and likely Australian skipper), allowed the English team such a long look at Higgs – but Brearley and co. didn't complain about that.

Meanwhile over in New Zealand, Kerry Packer's efforts to take his brand of cricket to other countries was meeting with little success. The weather has ruined several matches and the others have been played on bad pitches in front of poor crowds.

November 15

GOWER A one-day match at Canberra against a New South Wales Country XI. A dubious wicket but both Fiery and Tolly get good hundreds. Good to see Tolly do well because his cricket is likely to be limited over the next few weeks unless he forces his way through as a batter. Fiery's knee appeared to hold up well in his innings and Tolly seemed to galvanize him into playing his shots. A mate of mine from Perth takes Tolly, Arkle and myself to a very pleasant eating spot overlooking one of Canberra's valleys. A nice change to get away from hotel restaurants.

Next day it's off to Sydney. An early start (7.45) and by 2 pm we're having nets in Sydney. They're not very well prepared and of dubious value. Then it's off to drinks and a buffet, courtesy of the New South Wales Cricket Association. A few stars from yesteryear attend – Sir Len Hutton, Alan Davidson, Arthur Morris. Later on, I take a stroll down the road outside our hotel.

It's the infamous King's Cross area, Sydney's equivalent to Soho. Prostitutes, blue movies, garish lights – not paying for anything!

November 17

TAYLOR   The match against New South Wales begins. Bob Willis, captaining the side for the first time on the tour, wins the toss and we bat on a good wicket. Randall gets a good hundred and Botham – in his first match – a typically aggressive fifty. Geoff Miller takes six wickets and bowls very well – I'm pleased for him because he's working hard at his game, thinking it all out and giving the ball a lot more flight. Confidence is always a bit of a problem with Dusty – sometimes he has too much of it but most of the time he lacks it. This performance will have done him good.

In the evening Goose and I had dinner with an old friend, Dr Arthur Jackson and his wife, Anne, in a very unusual Chinese restaurant. The lift had a perspex window and as soon as we were above ground level we could see all over Sydney as we travelled to the roof-top restaurant. A lovely evening – Arthur is a hypnotherapist and he's helped Goose a lot with tapes he's sent him in the last two years. Goose plays the tapes when he needs to relax and they've made him a calmer, more mature person and undoubtedly helped his bowling. If I felt I needed them, I'd use Arthur's tapes as well; I was amazed how relaxed I felt when I played one. In fact I was so relaxed that the chambermaid was very embarrassed when she walked into my room!

GOWER   Gooch and Randall did well to survive early pressure from the lively Lawson and they put on 125 for the second wicket. I was stuffed completely by the leg-spinner Hourn's quicker ball – he bowled it straight for once and I'm out for 26.

November 18

Willis a more forceful captain in the field than Brearley. Superficially he doesn't seem as easygoing as Brears. The day goes well, all the catches are taken and I caught Toohey over my head at cover after we'd tied him down outside the off-stump by using a gully (Boycs of all people) and a short point. He finally lost patience. I know how he felt . . .

Feeling very weary at the moment. Getting up in the mornings is becoming difficult again. Thinking of taking things easy up to the Test in a fortnight's time. If selected, I don't want to be asleep on the feet . . .

November 19

We enforce the follow-on after forty minutes' play but the rain starts at 2 pm and doesn't stop. The cards come out and I join in with Dusty, Embers, Zap and Mike Gatting, who's over here on a Whitbread scholarship and helping us out in the nets as a bowler. Over dinner we discuss different batting techniques to be used in Australia, especially how to get used to leaving anything that's pitched short and which will therefore bounce over the wickets. Naturally the bowlers in our company reckon the batsmen should make millions, especially as the ball gets soft quickly. But we batsmen are more concerned with how easy or otherwise it is to change one's basic way of playing. And there's the extra complication of the lack of bounce on most of the wickets we've encountered in the first month – a very un-Australian phenomenon.

November 20

TAYLOR   A beautiful day after the storm. We work hard to bowl out NSW and we just fail to win by an innings. We only need four to win and Alan Lawson bowls four bouncers in a row at Boycs. The last one flew off his gloves over slips for the winning runs. Tom Brooks, the umpire, warned Lawson after the second bouncer but he took no notice. It looks as if the Aussies will be gunning for Boycs from now on. Ian Botham made a fine comeback, taking five wickets to add to his fifty. There was one amusing moment when, with just one NSW wicket to fall, John Emburey jokingly banged his spikes onto a spinner's length on the wicket. Graham Gooch shouted out, quite seriously, 'Hold on a bit, Embers, I've got to bat on that' – even though they were only a couple of runs ahead!

That evening we flew out to Brisbane and at Sydney Airport bumped into Packer's players en route from New Zealand and on their way to Perth. We all shook hands and talked for a while. Rod

Marsh told me the wickets had been diabolical and Derek Randall gave Clive Rice a playful poke in the ribs that made him wince. Arkle didn't know that the previous day Dennis Lillee hit Clive on that spot and cracked two of his ribs!

GOWER   It was the first time we'd met the Packer players on the tour but, as one would expect, there were no problems. It was simply a case of saying 'hello' to friends and colleagues from home and meeting a few other well-known cricketers. Nevertheless any official contact would be frowned upon.

Managed to fit in a television recording wishing Graham McKenzie well for his testimonial dinner in Perth. It was a programme rather on the lines of 'This is Your Life' back home. Brears and Boycs also recorded their greetings to Garth. It was strange that they picked me, because although we played together at Leicester, I only knew him very briefly for just one season.

Flew to Brisbane and had a conversation with Doug Insole and Brears about batting techniques and attitudes, etc. A casual reminder of my responsibilities, designed to confirm that we've got a battle on our hands over here. They told me I mustn't keep getting forty or fifty and then getting out playing a rash shot. They said this series wouldn't be as easy for me as the previous two against Pakistan and New Zealand. It wasn't a rollicking, more a conversation aimed at encouraging me – something we all need at some stage.

MURPHY   Many were alarmed at Lawson's bouncer attack on Boycott. The feeling persisted that it was launched on behalf of the Australian Test squad to see how England's premier batsman would cope with systematic short-pitched bowling. Doug Insole pointed out that the threat of banning Lawson from the rest of the second innings was irrelevant because there were only four runs needed to win. So Lawson had nothing to lose. Fears were expressed in the media that a bumper war could break out, but the hope was that Brearley could win the series easily enough without over-dependence on bumpers.

Lawson's folly only served to overshadow his fine bowling in the first innings. He looked hostile, bowled some very good, selective bouncers – twice Botham took cover on the ground – and at twenty-one looked a very good prospect, better than the twenty-seven-year-old Rodney Hogg with the suspect stamina . . . or so it seemed at the time. In the event Hogg blossomed while Lawson faded into anonymity. The England fielding was again good and Botham's all-round qualities were impressively displayed for the first time on the tour. His Australian-style aggression would surely be invaluable in the coming months. Peter Toohey, Australia's best batsman, was twice dismissed cheaply, on each occasion shrewd field placings proving decisive. The decision by Willis to enforce the follow-on proved correct because his bowlers gained some much-needed match practice.

Altogether an encouraging game for England – Randall assured his Test place with a fine hundred, and Gooch battled well for his 66. But Radley still struggled and Gower was showing a tendency to throw away his wicket when well set. On this tour, with so few chances of an innings, every opportunity had to be taken. Fortunately for England, Gower's best days were still to come.

November 22

GOWER Enjoyable 35-over game at Bundaberg against a Queensland Country XI. My duties not very arduous – I'm twelfth man taking out the drinks on the warmest day of the tour. Brears, Tolly, Arkle and Zap all get attractive runs. The opposition stronger than other country games, they include a couple of State players and some former State men. Blood on the pitch again – Scott Ledger, one of their openers, was hit on both sides of the head by JK and Hendo. He picked up a few stitches but was still smiling at the end. At the reception afterwards we were all presented with some samples of 'the famous Bundaberg rum' and cane-cutter replicas. Definite sugar area!

All of us in good spirits on the flight back, but at the hotel felt restless after not a very busy day. Took refuge with a couple of others in the disco downstairs, but the music wasn't so good and I eventually retired, not so gracefully and a little bit the worse for wear!

November 24

Back to the bouncy nets at Brisbane's Church of England School –
great practice for trying to adapt to the alleged local conditions.
Warm and humid; the school pool's just the job at midday! In the
afternoon, Dusty, Zap and I make for the hairdressing salon. The
demon barber does a fair job, although judging by the events of
the next few days he seems to have sapped this particular
Samson's strength . . .

November 24

TAYLOR   The Queensland game begins. The wicket looks green
and hard and it's been prepared by the same groundsman who
looks after the Church of England School wickets we've practised
on. These wickets are quicker than anything we've played on so
far with plenty of bounce. More and more of our lads are talking of
wearing helmets when they bat. We lose the toss and much to our
surprise they decide to bat and they're all out for 172. I drop
Ogilvie (five Tests for Australia) – I should have left the snick for
Mike Brearley at slip – but I take three catches. Another batsman's hit on the head – Ogilvie misjudged a short one from Goose
which wasn't a bouncer, and needed stitches. Our bowlers pitched
a little short and perhaps Queensland should have been out for
less because we also dropped several catches.

Boycott's bad run continues – he was out, caught at slip for just 6
off twenty-one-year-old Brabon, who was playing for the Country
XI two days earlier (the first time in thirty years that a player's
made a straight leap from country to State cricket). This dismissal
earned the Queensland side about £600 because a local firm had
offered the prize money if Fiery was out for less than 20 runs.

MURPHY   Perhaps Boycott had other more pressing matters on
his mind. That day he issued two statements – one accusing the
Yorkshire committee of a smear campaign against him in order to
retain power and later he offered to lead his county for another
two years. He said that if in that time he failed to win a major
trophy, he'd happily stand down and play under any captain. The
day began with the committee's statement that some players

would leave the club if Boycott was re-instated. With Boycott failing to get behind the line of the ball for the second time in a week (elementary stuff for a batsman of his model technique against modest bowling), it was easily the Yorkshireman's worst day of the tour so far. And the worry for England was that his private nightmare still seemed far from over . . .

GOWER   At the end of the first day, we had a surprise meeting in the team room to celebrate the birthdays of Kenny Barrington and Guy. The hotel management laid on champagne and two sponge cakes shaped like cricket bats. Then Zap, Rad and I dragged Dusty out to a recommended Italian restaurant but we hadn't booked and we ended up back at the hotel. Brears and Doug Insole joined us, but the manager kept being summoned to the hotel reception – the media getting concerned again about Boycs.

November 25
Trevor MacDonald of ITN at the ground with a camera crew looking for, you've guessed it, Boycs. I'm out, yorked for 6, not feeling in magic form. I struck the ball well in the nets during the afternoon with Goochy throwing a few down and whistling them round the old earholes. Another batsman hit on the head – Walters, the opener, ducks into the only bouncer given him by Goose and he's sent to hospital for more stitches. Blood getting to be a common sight on cricket grounds these days – the fifth headwound we've witnessed in a month. Makes one wonder if we are actually playing a sensible game any more. Anyway the bouncy wicket's more of a challenge than I've had to face recently. I'm just hoping I can find some form before the Test.
TAYLOR   Next day we let Queensland off the hook. We had them two down for nought plus an opener in hospital and not likely to bat again, yet their last five wickets put on 200 runs. John Maclean, who'll keep wicket for Australia next week, scored 94 in three hours and hit the ball very hard. Ogilvie, who was hit on the head by Willis in the first innings, wore a white crashhelmet and looked in no trouble. The events of the last few days have made

most of us decide to wear a crashhelmet in the Test on this ground. They're coloured blue and made by a firm that manufactures horse-riding gear. They have a peaked cap and perspex on the side to protect the temples. Everyone likes them and, with the wickets playing so unpredictably, who can blame us for wearing them?

November 27

GOWER   We make 208, to win by six wickets despite my contribution – one run. I'm out off a mistimed cut and take things seriously enough to have another net when the game ends. Arkle – fresh from his success the night before when the locals dedicated a song to him at a barbecue and he gave them his cabaret act in return – again batted well for 113 runs in the match.

Interesting evening at a French restaurant. Rad, Zap, Brears, Doug Insole and I eat outside and although the overall cost – with a few bottles of red wine thrown in – exceeds the meal allowance, it was a nice quiet evening without any bowlers present! This ensures that when cricket is discussed, it can be concentrated solely on the batsman's point of view!

The next day's a free one – free that is from nets and training. In the morning eight of us do some PR work at a store in association with 4IP Radio (a local station) and in the afternoon, Hendo, Dusty, Henri, Embers, Zap, Bernie Thomas and I play golf. I only play nine holes, manage five over par, must be the best figures of my life. Drinks with the Governor General in the evening. Not the worst function because I pass the time chatting to one of his daughters and avoid the usual earbashing.

November 29

Our team's announced for the Test. It's the same as that which played against Queensland. I'm relieved to be in, though there are still some doubts at the back of my mind over my form.

On to a reception with the Lord Mayor. Have to listen for hours to talk about youth cricket. Afterwards I test out the main hotel restaurant and have a bit of pheasant. A pleasant change from the standard Aussie grub, although it takes a chunk out of the wallet!

November 30

D-Day minus one! The nets feel good and I'm encouraged. I test out the helmet I'm going to wear. This type's been used recently by the Packer players and if great batsmen like Ian Chappell feel they should be worn, then it makes even more sense for me to wear one. If it helps my confidence, what have I got to lose? Every now and again an unplayable bouncer arrives and you're in trouble.

The usual pre-Test dinner. Lots of banter but also serious discussion about the opposition's strengths and weaknesses. I'm taking things as easy as possible – saving up the strength for the big one!

MURPHY England went into the First Test 11/8-on favourites with Australia quoted at 7/2. The odds seemed harsh on Australia, considering England's uncertain form, but a team with 256 caps compared with 55 obviously had the edge in experience. Only Kim Hughes and Gary Cosier had played Test cricket against England – once each and 15 runs between them. Much would depend on England blunting the pace attack of Hogg and Hurst, and Mike Brearley predicted that the pitch would be fast and green with variable bounce. Bob Willis thought the game would be over in four days and that pace bowling would hold the key to the series, a forecast overturned to a degree by the consistency of Miller and Emburey, the England off-spinners.

Much of the pre-Test talk was about bumpers and the new protective headgear, but it was felt that Hogg and co. wouldn't over-indulge because Willis and Botham were fully capable of retaliation. This time the forecast proved correct.

Brearley – with a tour batting average of 140 – will bat at number 4. He said it would be an unjustified panic measure to move Gooch down the order and that the batting line-up would be better balanced with the captain following Randall and preceding Gower. Soon Brearley had to change his mind . . .

The series was opening against the background of the spectacular success of Kerry Packer's night cricket in Sydney. Two days before, 44,000 spectators had watched a fifty-over match under the Sydney floodlights between Australia and the West Indies, and the fact that the cricket was dull didn't deter the World Series publicity machine from greeting the evening with hysterical forecasts. Not everyone welcomed the evening's entertainment – residents from as far as three miles away claimed the new floodlights swamped their homes with light, bus drivers claimed that louts vandalized their buses and hurled beer cans into gardens.

But the Packer organization were happy to deal in figures and quote crowd statistics – a sobering thought for the traditional brand of cricket as another Ashes series got under way . . .

3
Brisbane – First Test

TAYLOR Arrive at the ground at 9.15. Practice and then it's a ceremony commemorating fifty years of Test cricket at the Gabba. A skydiver parachutes down and we all get commemorative medals. Seemed a little contrived to me, it felt like a Packer-style gimmick to amuse the crowds. We're very nervous in the dressing room – we had no idea how good the new breed of Aussies were and time after time people would come up to us at receptions and say, 'We're a very young side, you won't have much to beat.' That was always taken with a pinch of salt because these Aussies can find Test players from anywhere – four years ago, Jeff Thomson was a nobody and he went on to shatter Mike Denness' side. Brears said the first hour would be vital and it was a good toss to lose because our out-cricket was excellent. Lulu runs out Cosier in the first over, our confidence is boosted straight away and we've got them on the run!

They seem to lack application – Kim Hughes chases a wide one and gives me a straightforward catch and Laughlin hooks one down fine-leg's throat. They're 26 for 6 at one stage and we couldn't believe it at lunchtime – Brears tells us to keep our heads down and whittle out the other four batters and, although Hogg and Maclean get a few runs, this is what we do. Hoggy walks in to bat with his new white helmet on, I passed a remark about it and he said, 'I don't care what I look like, I'm scared stiff!' Odd for someone to be so honest . . .

I get five catches, equalling the England record in an innings against Aussie, but they weren't special. They went straight in and stayed. In fact I didn't feel at the top of my form; it took me a while to get into the swing of things.

When we bat, Goochy is given out, apparently caught off his thigh pad and then with forty minutes to go. Boycs is out for the third time running to Hoggy. I go in as nightwatchman to face a barrage of short-pitched stuff from Hurst and Hogg. As I walk in, I'm telling myself not to push forward too much to them because I'm a recognized batter and they can bounce me. I'll be on the back foot waiting for it. The helmet's a great psychological boost and I was happy just to stay there watching Arkle play some fine shots. Randall's an amazing character – when it's his turn to bat he jumps up, says 'Come on, England, come on, England' to himself a few times just to psych himself up, and then rushes out. This is the first time I've batted with him and he's giving Hoggy the verbals ('Come on, you . . ., bounce the . . ., I'll smash you') but it's all nerves.

GOWER   My run-out of Cosier was a matter of inches. They'd been looking to drop the ball just in front of them and run for a quick single, so the old adrenalin was pumping extra and I was a little nearer to the batters. It was an excellent bowling performance and the fielders carried out Brears' instructions and supported them well. Goose takes four wickets; like the rest of us he was really keyed up – he got Toohey with a good one that came back a bit as he tried a rather loose drive. Surprised to see Boycs out, his whole philosophy of batting revolves round occupation and he looked well set. The crowd disappointing – the ground would only have been half full but for a large number of schoolkids.

In the evening, absolutely shattered. There's something special about the first day of the series, you get mentally drained because the atmosphere's been building up for some time. A new experience for me to play in a Test abroad.

Second day

TAYLOR   Brears tells us to play our natural game. I do and decide to stay there, but Arkle struggles. We try to wear down Hurst and Hogg but the crowd gets on to Arkle and they help get him out – he loses patience and slashes one to gully. I feel comfortable in my helmet, bat three hours for 20 and get called a Pommie without a father by the crowd – among other things! My tactics justified though, because the Aussies didn't have a class third-seamer in conditions that favoured them, so Lulu and Both had the platform to give them a tonking later on. Hogg impressed me – he's like Statham in the way that he bowls so straight, you give up waiting for half volleys! Hurst didn't seem as quick as a few years back when I played with him in South Africa for the International Wanderers. On that tour he hit Barry Richards in the face and he looked very sharp. He's slower now but seems to have learned some craft.

Lulu and Both hit the ball hard and we end the day 141 ahead with three wickets left. The helmet seems to have done Lulu some good as well – he'd looked wary of the short-pitched stuff before, but now he seemed full of confidence.

GOWER The helmet didn't worry me and it was nice to know that if I *did* get something wrong, it was there for protection. I didn't feel as nervous walking in to bat as I did in my first Test in England. This one was just a continuation of the tour, more like a county XI, whereas at home, you turn up from your own county and have to blend very quickly. In my partnership with Both the ball seemed to come onto the bat quite nicely and I felt good after Hogg's first over with the new ball when I hit one off the back foot through cover. Both was highly amused when he was hit on the head, he tapped his helmet and laughed heartily!

Disappointed to get out, caught behind when set, but it could have been worse. Some interesting umpiring decisions during the day – could be a feature of the series. Overall they seem to have evened themselves out, but one day's decisions might not. Stay at the ground after the close of play and Chilly, Both and I have a few grogs with the opposition.

Third day
TAYLOR We lead by 170 and Goose again gives us a great start, bowling Cosier through the gate first ball. Goose does his war dance . . . Both gets Toohey LBW and they're 2 for 2! You can't go wrong if you get a wicket in the first over in both innings of a Test! I catch Yallop off Goose when he's scored 19 but the umpire doesn't hear the fine edge – it's very windy at that time, it's

blowing in the umpire's face and it *was* a fine edge. But I could tell from Yallop's face he'd nicked it, he went to walk, then checked and stayed his ground.

Kim Hughes plays well, it was a controlled knock and he wasn't as overawed by the occasion as he was on his Test debut against us in 1977. That time, Goose and Brears told us, he took over an hour to make one run and looked completely out of his class. Now he showed a good temperament and his six to square-leg off Goose was a beauty . . .

They end up just 13 runs short with 7 wickets left. Must make an early breakthrough when play resumes because we have to bat last.

GOWER   Yallop hit some good shots off the back foot and played the spinners particularly well. He doesn't pull but is a good, hard cutter. Hughes plays forward a lot and tends to run at the ball. When he's finished his shot, he's still on the move. He's a good hooker because he seems to pick the ball up early but he *does* hit it in the air. We set a trap for him – a fine-leg and myself at deep square-leg for the hook, but so far it hasn't worked.

Rest day tomorrow so the lads take the opportunity of relaxing. Certainly not many hold back on the Castlemaine 4X – only recently available after the Biisbane beer strike.

Rest day

TAYLOR   Eight of us drive to Surfers' Paradise, south of Brisbane, but the weather not too kind and just after lunch return in a tropical storm. We have to stop on the side of the road because the rain's too heavy. One worry – an air strike is starting, which threatens the tour itinerary. Ansett Airlines handle our internal flights in Aussie and their rep says the Air Force might have to take us to Perth after the Test – or, failing that, it's a three-day journey there across the desert, perish the thought!

GOWER   The rain made it a good time for a rest day. Off to a beach forty miles north of Brisbane with Scyld Berry of *The Observer* (good press relations?!) and the wind created a desert-type sandstorm. Quite an impressive sight when the storm broke, although the windscreen wipers packing up on the car didn't help.

Bob Taylor tests out an Austin Seven in Brisbane on the day before the first
Test (*photo*: *Bernard Thomas*)

Some of the England party watching the first Test at Brisbane: (left to right)
Edmonds, Tolchard, Randall, a room attendant, Hendrick and Gower (*photo*:
Ron McKenzie/News Ltd, Sydney)

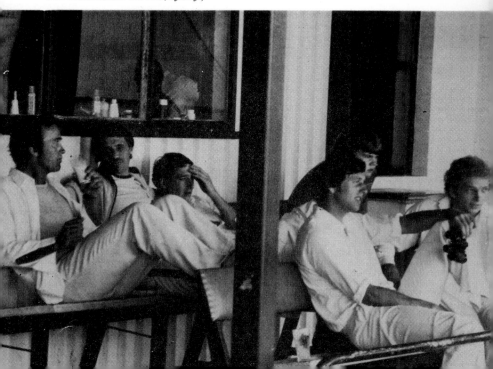

Two examples of run-outs by David Gower – the first (above) to dismiss
Laughlin in the Victoria match at Melbourne and then (below) at Brisbane in the
first Test when Cosier is out in the first over (*photos: Ron McKenzie/News Ltd, Sydney*)

Two dodgy moments for David Gower during his century in the second Test at Perth – (above) he's almost run out by the wicket-keeper, MacLean, and (below) Hogg hits him on the neck (*photos: Patrick Eagar*)

David Gower has just completed his first Test hundred against Australia with a boundary off Hurst at Perth in the second Test – and Geoff Boycott's on hand to add his congratulations (*photo: Ron McKenzie/News Ltd, Sydney*)

It's all smiles for skipper Brearley ̶ after the second Test has been won (*photo: Patrick F͘*

No danger of sunburn. Didn't think much about the cricket; it normally depends on how immediate my contribution is likely to be next day.

Fourth day

TAYLOR   Very hot and sultry. Struggle to chip away at them and finally we're set 169 to win. Dusty bowls very well – 34 overs of flight and variation, not so flat as he normally bowls in Tests and he looked a better bowler because of it. Playing in the First Test ahead of Embers has done his confidence a lot of good, because he was dropped in favour of Embers in the last Test in England against New Zealand. He also has a bit of a complex about Jim Laker saying in the press that he doesn't flight the ball and he was worried about not making many runs. This performance will have done him a lot of good.

Henri has words with Brears. The breeze was helping Dusty's off-spin more than Henri's left-armers and his reaction in the field seemed to indicate he wasn't happy. When he finally came on, he told me in a loud voice as I threw the ball back to him that he was going to bowl a bouncer. I was sure the Aussie batsmen had heard him and sure enough, there was John Maclean at the bowler's end telling Bruce Yardley what was coming up. I motioned to Henri to forget it as he started running in, but he took no notice and I didn't have a price as the ball shot past my left shoulder for four byes. I wasn't pleased because I don't like giving away byes. He only bowled 12 overs in the innings.

GOWER   A good performance to niggle away at ┆   ┆e realized it would be hard work for the bowlers and the h┆ ┆ers knew they mustn't get slack or lazy if wickets aren't falling. Mills bowled tight and well, but Henri didn't look too penetrative. Yallop and Hughes both get hundreds and play well in their different ways. Boycs and Zap survive a tricky last forty-five minutes and the only question mark now is: how much will the ball turn tomorrow?

In the evening the first of our Perkins Engines receptions. In return for the money they put into our pool, we turn up at several functions and meet their clients and their own executives. Good PR and mutually beneficial.

Fifth day

TAYLOR   We stroll home by seven wickets, but not before some nasty moments. Goochy goes early and then Arkle runs out Boycs! He called Boycs for a quick single and Toohey threw the stumps down from cover – a great bit of fielding. Remembering how Fiery had run out Arkle at Trent Bridge against the Aussies in 1977, I said 'that's one-all now' but the dressing room was very quiet. In the last innings, 169 takes some getting and it was in the back of my mind that we'd had them 26 for 6 on the first morning and perhaps we'd made hard work of it since . . .

Brears gets out at 74 for 3 and in strolls Lulu. An ideal man to go in at that time, he's so calm. In the dressing room he'll join in the chat even if he's next man in – nothing seems to worry him. He plays his best knock of the tour, Randall prospers and we win easily. We celebrate with champagne and the Aussies join us (before the Test started, we'd decided it was up to the individual player whether he wanted to socialize with the Aussies every night because some of us usually wanted to get back to the hotel; Yallop was quite agreeable). The Aussies a good social bunch – Bruce Yardley's a funny man, with a good impersonation of a Lancastrian accent and a nice line in song and dancer patter. John Maclean's a nice fellow, although Graham Wood's a bit of a 'show pony' – he struts around a bit and likes to be in the limelight.

In the evening, eight of us go to see Harry Secombe's show. He's godfather to Kenny Barrington's son, loves his cricket and a smashing bloke. Backstage it's an amazing sight – about fifteen people are in his dressing room that's no bigger than a hotel lift, and there's Harry in the middle of it all, with a champagne bottle in his hand, loving every minute of it!

GOWER   A rewarding feeling to win so well and nice for me to get a few more runs – and a not-out for a change! Played better than in the first innings, I was more controlled. The spinners were turning it a little and I hung on till lunch and then hit a few afterwards. My best knock of the tour so far. A good laugh near the end when Hoggy's bowling to Randall:

Hogg: (after bowling a wide one) 'Come on you Pommie bastard, hit that.'

Randall: (jumping up and down) 'Come on, you . . ., bounce it, bounce it!'

In the evening a quick dive into the pool and then I just fancy a quiet night with some music and a wine cask. Won't be long before we're on the job again (cricket, I mean), so might as well make the most of the relaxation.

First Test reflections

TAYLOR We're not fooled by the result. We know the Aussies have some talented young batsmen and that one day they'll come good together. Hogg and Hurst looked sharp and dangerous and Hogg's asthma certainly hadn't affected his stamina. In retrospect we were perhaps lucky they batted first. It gave us a chance to show how good our out-cricket was, instead of our rather brittle batting.

It's funny how players change from season to season. Looking at the first six Aussie batters before the Test, I picked out Cosier as the danger man. He'd made a hundred against the West Indies in his first Test and he's a dangerous attacking player. Yet he made one run in two innings and didn't look Test class. Everyone had been raving about Toohey – yet we'd noticed in the State game how he plays in the air off the back foot, making him vulnerable in the gully and point area.

We were all pleased with our helmets. I shan't be without one for the rest of my career whenever I bat and it was amazing to see how confident our lads looked. Boycs and Arkle say they won't wear them but I think that's just pride . . .

I wasn't too impressed with Yallop's captaincy in the field. He had this idea of a rota at first slip involving himself, Hughes and Cosier – yet Cosier's a specialist with Queensland. Surely a Test player has the mental stamina to stand at slip all day? I couldn't understand why Yallop didn't use the leg-spin of Higgs against me and Arkle on the second morning. We weren't scoring much against the speed stuff but we were reasonably comfortable. I far prefer playing the fast men rather than the leg-spinners because we don't see many of them in England and during the changeover I'd say to Arkle, 'Surely he'll bring on Higgsy now?' and Arkle would say, 'Shut up, Yallop might hear you.'

At the end of the match the Aussie selectors announced the team for the next Test – something I don't agree with, because surely they need time to reflect on the match that's just finished rather than announce the side straight away? Anyway they've dropped Higgs, which surprised me, brought in the left-arm swing bowler Dymock (that's not a bad selection because Hogg and Hurst need support) and picked Darling – that's a selection for us, because we got him out cheaply twice in the game against South Australia and we think our quickies will take care of him.

So we're quite happy – but we've got a few of our own problems. Goochy had a bad match with the bat and he dropped a couple of catches, Boycs still isn't himself and we're all worried about Goose's feet. They look in a terrible state and although he doesn't say much, I know he's in a lot of pain. Lots of old ladies are offering him recipes and cures and I hope one of them works because this game again showed how much we need him.

GOWER   We did well to win so easily, but we're under no illusions. We don't think the Aussies are easy meat – Yallop and Hughes have shown they can bat, I saw Wood get a fine hundred last year in the Gillette Cup Final (and he made good runs in the West Indies) and Toohey can play a bit. There's still the feeling that if our batting lets us down our bowlers might have a lot of work to do.

Hoggy looked impressive and his asthma trouble didn't affect him. In fact I think this asthma thing has been blown up out of proportion – the day he bowled against us for South Australia, it was very stuffy and the pollen count was high. Anyone with just a sniffle would have suffered.

Hurst is slower than Hogg but can swing it and bowl a quicker one. He got me with one in the first innings, just after I'd square-cut him to the boundary. He put a little more into the next ball, it bounced more and I edged it to the keeper. So they're a good pair of strike bowlers and Dymock's selection for the next Test will boost that department. I'm surprised they've dropped Higgs, because from what I know of the Perth wicket, the extra bounce would've helped him. But I suppose the final place was between him and Yardley, and Yardley's batting was probably decisive.

There'd been some talk about Brears opening with Boycs in the next Test, but as far as I was concerned that was nonsense. Zap had simply had a bad match and there was no need to panic after one Test.

I was pleased with my helmet and with the confidence it gave me. I hadn't been really worried about my form (after all, the Tests *are* the important games) but I'd had a few extra nets and the one the day before the Test started had been a particularly good one. Now for a crack at that Perth wicket!

MURPHY England's experience was one of the decisive factors. They capitalized on the English-style conditions on that first morning and never really let go of the match. Yallop's field placing and general control of affairs compared unfavourably with Brearley's grasp of things, but it was generally felt that this young Australian side could only get better.

Lack of concentration continued to be an Australian weakness throughout the series – Hughes' careless swish with the score 24 for 4 epitomized his batting throughout the series. Time after time this fine player would be on the verge of establishing mastery – but then he'd lose concentration and throw his wicket away. Toohey was never a force – his undistinguished batting in this match continued throughout the series, apart from one knock at Perth, and he was dropped for the Fifth Test. The England bowlers had noticed some imperfections in his technique in the New South Wales match and they were characteristically merciless in exploiting them. They also noticed Maclean's weakness against off-spin in this Test. Miller haunted him for the next three Tests and eventually it was Maclean's inability to make any runs as much as his defects behind the stumps that led to his omission.

It was the last Test of the series for Edmonds and Old. The Yorkshireman never managed to shrug off his niggling injuries and the success of Emburey and Miller as off-spinners left the talented Edmonds on the sidelines. For Boycott, the poor footwork he displayed in this Test proved to be a depressingly common occurrence, and apart from a valuable holding operation at Perth, the side had to soldier on without a major innings from its senior batsman. There *were* consolations – Gower continued to beguile the spectators and score consistently and Randall, technical imperfections notwithstanding, became a valuable number three batsman. Gooch also struggled – his poor performance in Brisbane didn't exactly give way to blue skies in later Tests (despite some dubious umpiring decisions against him) and when the captain bowed to the inevitable and moved up the order to open the innings, Gooch's figures weren't dramatically improved.

In fact, with Willis never again a decisive influence after Perth, England continued to be individually vulnerable – but frustratingly for Australia, their teamwork and leadership hardly ever faltered.

4
Perth – Second Test

December 7

GOWER Fly out to Perth in the afternoon. Certain sense of excitement going back to the place where I spent four happy months last year. Unlike the rest of Australia, it's a place I know, the people are friendly and I'm looking forward to seeing a few friends. Hit the beaches again as soon as we get there and make full use of a van lent to me by my mate, Nick Duncan.

TAYLOR It takes seven hours to get to Perth, just shows you what a huge country this is. On the flight, Both gives JK the usual legpull (JK doesn't like flying and sits there fairly quietly), some of us play cards, Guy uses his waterpistol to full irritating effect, Brears reads or talks tactics with Goose, the manager and Kenny. Arkle starts singing 'Rule Britannia' all of a sudden and I wish the flight was over! Boycs sits writing all the time – when we're batting in the Tests he wants a complete account of every ball bowled by the Aussies. It's for his book of the tour and he's fanatical about it. In the last Test he got people to stand in for him when he was at the toilet – and it's not just, for example, 'no run', it's got to be 'Hurst bowls outside the off stump, no shot from Taylor' and stuff like that! An amazing man . . .

It's about 107 degrees when we arrive – hope it's not like this during the Test. The flies are a problem too; I tell the others the Aussie salute is a wave across the face to get rid of the flies . . .

December 8

Long reception at the Mayor's Parlour. After being introduced we all have to stand up and bow – feel a right charlie. The Mayor tells us in his speech how Western Australia were going to thrash us because they hadn't lost a game in three years, and how good a skipper John Inverarity was compared with Yallop. More speeches, but afterwards I was lucky because I had a nice chat with the New Zealand High Commissioner and his English-born wife.

In the evening more nonsense from Randall. The two of us go crab and prawn fishing with Both and his friend, and we're wading through waist-high water, dragging our nets, when Arkle falls down a pot hole and lets all his catch go. It could only happen to him . . . We boiled our catch and had a lovely meal of prawns, crab and Fosters and Swans beer.

GOWER   At the Civic reception, the Opposition Leader becomes yet another to mispronounce Doug Insole's name. He's been described as 'Instole' and this time it's 'Ingersoll' – can it be that difficult? We end up calling him Drug Ingersoll, which appealed to his dry wit. Meet up with some of my old mates from the Claremont and Cottesloe Club I played with last year, and with county cricketers Jim Love, Chris Tavare, Geoff Humpage and Kevin Sharp, also out in Perth coaching and playing. The occasion is celebrated with a few beers . . .

December 9
Start of game against Western Australia. Diabolical wicket – it seams and bounces and zips through low on occasions. A lottery – what will it be like in next week's Test? I'm out first ball, trying to play a ball of fullish length past mid-off and nicking it to the keeper. If the ball's well up to me, I'll try to play it away every time – why change if it's the first ball?

In the circumstances, Tolly's 61 not out in a total of 144 was tremendous. He rode his luck but he *made* a lot of it, he improvised well and his footwork was superb. One of their blokes took an amazing catch to dismiss Both – he ran forty yards looking over his shoulder with the ball swirling behind him and ended up catching it inches off the ground. I've never seen anything like it.

When they bat, Hendo bowls immaculately. Test players like Wood, Hughes, Inverarity and Yardley can't lay a bat on him and JK has Wood in all sorts of trouble – a pointer to next week's Test?

Next day it's all over and we win easily with a day to spare. A good performance, especially from our bowlers, but I would've liked more match practice. I can't play in nets because I can't do the same things as in the middle; you play the shot, then have to throw back the ball and the next one's on you before you've had time to reflect on the previous one and get ready. You can have different sorts of bowlers in the nets as well – some pace, some spin, some left-handers and you have to keep changing your technique.

MURPHY   England's out-cricket contined to impress but this match again showed the fragility of the batting. Tolchard played the kind of quick-footed innings one associates with him and his claims for inclusion in the Test side were being loudly canvassed in some quarters. But the make-up of the side meant he didn't get in (and his frustrating tour reached its nadir when he fractured his cheekbone in the game at Newcastle in January).

Other points from the Western Australia match – young Kevin Wright looked a neat wicket-keeper and eventually he was to oust Maclean from the Test side. Lever's good bowling against Wood won him a place in the following week's Test team. But the real talking point was, again, Boycott – and not because he'd twice failed with the bat. He'd been reported by one of the umpires for swearing during the match and over the weekend he learned that a specially convened meeting of Yorkshire members had failed to return the captaincy to him.

GOWER   I was at mid-wicket and Boycs was at cover when an LBW appeal was turned down. Although it was windy, I could clearly hear him swear at the umpire. He was under a lot of pressure, he thought he'd been stuffed over a dubious LBW when batting and something just snapped. I felt a certain amount of sympathy for him, although I hope I never get in his position. He also has no confidence in his batting and his feet just weren't moving. I still think he'll come good but it was clearly getting him down. He's not the sort of person you press things with, you don't see much of him at night but then again he doesn't sit in his corner and say nothing. He's very good in team talks, he analyses opposition players' weaknesses well and I respect him. So far his relationship with Brears isn't too bad – there are some slight strains but Brears isn't one to hold a grudge and he does confer at times with Boycs.

TAYLOR   It wasn't like Fiery to blow his top like that at the umpire. We didn't talk about his problems openly but players have long memories and although I felt sorry for him with his mother dying, I reckon he had brought a lot of trouble on his own head. As a player it's very difficult to offer him advice – Kenny Barrington tried on the tour to Pakistan and New Zealand but Boycs didn't take much notice. On this tour other players in the opposing sides are telling Boycs he can't get the ball off the square and it was clearly getting to him. There were rumours about him flying home, but I don't believe it'll come to that. At the moment his suspicious mood is being reflected in his batting and I just hope he comes good soon. It'll be good for him and for the team . . .

December 13
A one-day game against the West Australian Country XI at Albany – and I'm the captain. Goose and Brears are rested and to my surprise I get the job. Boycs says to me, 'They're really kicking me when I'm down.' I told him I was surprised, 'But now I'm skipper, get down to fine leg!' He kept coming up and saying, 'How about a bowl?' I'd say, 'No, we're trying to win this match,' and his mood didn't improve. But Brears had told me he wanted Dusty and Henri to have a long bowl, so they had 14 overs each. Henri gets six wickets and we win easily and I'm presented with a pair of whales' teeth, mounted and inscribed 'Bob Taylor – captain of England'. I know it's only a minor game, but that can't be taken away from me.

December 14
GOWER   Practice for tomorrow's Test. We're going to play four pace bowlers and just one spinner, so Henri's out and JK plays. Chilly is declared unfit but Goose says his feet are better – he was fairly dry about it and discussed it mainly with Bernie Thomas.

Tonight we change our system on the eve of a Test and have the team talk before we eat. That way the meal can go on as long as we like after the discussion and there's time for a stroll or an early night. But there's still some hard talking done before the dinner – not least about the uncertainty of the Perth wicket and the talent in the Aussie side.

TAYLOR   We discussed Darling and his fondness for the hook shot, where to bowl to Yallop and Toohey (off stump), Wood's dodgy running between the wickets and how poorly Maclean played Dusty's off-breaks in the last Test. The general feeling was that Chilly should have declared himself fit – with a great team man like JK on hand, Chilly might regret his decision. We were desperate to get Goose fit. He was our main strike bowler and we knew some of the Aussies were scared of him. Some of the cures suggested were amazing – pure lamb's wool wrapped round the toes, hand cream, soft soap. I'm sure everyone means well but a local chiropodist seems to have done the trick with some sponge pads.

I watch some World Series Cricket on TV. Nothing exceptional and the players look fed up – Knotty looked really grubby with his white floppy hat almost threadbare and his pads falling apart. He'd altered his stance standing back, so that his hands were outside his pads and he didn't look his usual bouncy self. Derek Underwood seemed fed up as well. Without making too much of it, I've toured with these two many times and I can tell from their general attitude whether or not they're enjoying things – and they weren't tonight. The TV presentation was very good but the adverts after every over irritated me. Occasionally the camera caught an empty stand by mistake and quickly panned away to the populated areas. And the commentators! Fred Trueman kept saying 'that's the most magnificent catch/delivery/stroke you'll ever see' and Tony Cosier was the same – almost as if a Packer official was standing behind them all the time. At least Richie Benaud sounded neutral – he mentioned other cricket that had been played in Australia that day. The whole thing really did look like a circus to me and some of the comments made me want to throw up . . .

Second Test, first day

GOWER   My first hundred against Australia. Very, very satisfying feeling – but my thanks to Boycs who kept urging me on with sound commonsense. We're put in by Yallop. I think Brears would've done the same because it's overcast (is this really Perth?). The third wicket falls just after lunch, so the pressure's on again, although at that time, with the pitch helping the bowlers, 41 for 3 wasn't a bad score. As I go out to bat, my thoughts are on survival while still trying to play as naturally as possible. Hoggy is bowling fast and the first hour is fairly torrid – one hits me on the side of the neck and another flies wide of slip for four. Things get better as the day goes on and Boycs is holding up his end well, all the while chatting to me, helping me concentrate. Coming off at tea-time, Hogg says to me, 'You're a f . . . imposter, Gower,' because I'd played and missed a few times at him, but not to worry. Three times in a row, he beats me outside the off stick with the new ball – sharply lifting deliveries which move like off-breaks, but I keep plugging away. I reach my danger period in the fifties and tell myself to keep going. About half an hour before the close I think a century's possible. I shoot through the nineties, feeling calm enough and then five minutes from time, Hurst obliges with a ball on the leg stump. It goes sweetly off my bat through mid-on and I'm there. My first thoughts are that a hundred for England against Aussie mean so much, then I smile to myself at a newspaper report a few days earlier after I'd got a first-baller against Western Australia. 'Back to Cottesloe,' the bloke wrote – in other words, play a little more club cricket before batting for England . . .

Boycs and I shake hands and he has some generous things to say about me to the press. Arrange to go and see *Midnight Express* with some of the lads, but I had to get changed and I missed them. Went back to the hotel bar instead, sank a few celebratory drinks with Tavaré and the other English county players and end up well pleased. Bump into Bernie Thomas in the lift, can't find the words, wonder if he'll tell the manager about me having a few?

TAYLOR   Lulu didn't stop playing shots even near the end of the day when another player would've shut up shop and played for his hundred tomorrow. Again he showed his serene temperament because when he went in, Boycs was in all sorts of trouble and there wasn't much batting to come. But Lulu just played his normal way and although he had his luck (Hogg bowled really well at him) it was a magnificent knock. Full marks to Fiery as well – Dymock was still beating him outside the off-stump near the end of the day, but he never gave up and established the platform for Lulu's attacking innings.

I can't help feeling we would have done better if they'd batted first. If Brears had won the toss, we'd have put them in and with four seamers in our side, I wouldn't have given them much chance. If I were Yallop, I'd be a little dispirited tonight . . .

Second day

GOWER The morning training session soon got rid of my lethargy and I played sensibly for the first half-hour, adding just one run before Hogg bowled me with a beauty. Coming round the wicket, he bowled one that pitched off and hit off, and it was too fast for me to adjust. Fair enough . . .

Boycs grinds on to 77. He seems to have some trouble picking up Bruce Yardley's flight. At times he's deceptive, bowling a good quicker ball, but I felt confident facing him. He'd bowled well at Brisbane where the wicket offered more turn.

Dymock is a useful bowler – he changes his pace well, slips in the odd awkward bouncer and keeps the ball angling away from the right-hander, with the inswinger holding up as a useful alternative. To me the main concern is the one that might just nip away off the pitch, because it can be tempting to play a man of his pace through the covers off either foot when the ball's near the off-stump.

When they bat, JK shows Wood is his rabbit, getting him LBW. Brears gave him the new ball for this reason and he shared it with Guy, who tried to swing it. But the dry Perth atmosphere doesn't help him and Goose comes on and does the business with Hughes and Yallop being clean-bowled. Darling then runs himself out for some reason and, with four wickets down at the close, they're right in it . . .

TAYLOR   We got some stick from the crowd because we took a long time to get our runs after Lulu was out. I appreciate their feelings and I'm conscious of our duty to entertain, but they didn't realize how much the overcast conditions and green wicket favoured their seamers. Hoggy had a go at me because I was leaving a few outside the off-stump. He called me a 'Pommie . . .' I called him 'a big girl's blouse' and felt better for it. One worry – I strained my groin while batting and it really aches at night. I start taking pain killers and have treatment from Bernie Thomas.

One amusing moment when Goose clean-bowled Hughes; the delivery broke off the stump and left the triangular part in the ground and they had to send for the groundsman to cut it out. So poor old Yallop, the next man in, had to wait around for five minutes before he could take strike!

Third day

GOWER   Toohey (known to us as 'Rats' – get it? Ratatouille??) bats very well to carry his bat but there's little support for him. He straight-drives very well and hooks and pulls efficiently (as Both found out in one over when he was pitching short; Willis gave him a rocket for that over). He plays very much like Doug Walters, in other words attractively but riskily. Dusty gets Maclean again and with Zap and Boycs well set at the close, we're 167 ahead. The Aussies appeal a lot but by now we've accepted it and decided to do the same thing. The thinking was that we'd lose out otherwise, because by the law of averages, the more appeals the more chance of success.

TAYLOR   For the first time in my career I'm worried about an injury. I take three straightforward catches but when I move to the side I really struggle. It's murder down the leg-side, particularly to JK if he's bowling his left-arm stuff to a right-hand bat. But the bowlers knew my problems and generally bowled tightly.

Guy fancied Toohey with a bouncer. He's spotted some weakness against the short-pitched delivery but this time Toohey won the battle. Brears had a quiet word with Both and took him off; that's his way of captaincy, he doesn't bawl someone out in front of the rest of the side. Hoggy gets a dubious decision – Goose beat him for speed, the ball brushed his thigh, the slips appealed, but I didn't – yet he's given out caught by me!

Rest day

Trying to get my groin right for tomorrow with Bernie's help. Four sessions of electric pad treatment, beginning at 7.30 in the morning and finishing at 10.30 at night. Very worried, but Bernie a great encourager – a born optimist and a bit of a blarney boy when necessary.

Fourth day

GOWER We bat rather carelessly in the second innings. So many people go on about the need for quick runs that they forget you can easily lose a few wickets playing this way and give the game back to the opposition. I wasn't keyed-up enough and played a few air shots outside the off-stump which I like to think I wouldn't have done in the first innings. Finally Hogg gets me tucked up with a faster one and I nick it to the keeper. Brears gets a duck – nobody says anything in the dressing room. It's all been said before when people ask about the captain's batting; we still think he'll come good and apart from that he's a bloody good captain and therefore worth his place in the side.

In the end our target of 374 is a reasonable one, although the nagging thought remains that a couple of good partnerships would get them near victory.

TAYLOR Goochy seemed to be unlucky when given out LBW. He might well have been given out three balls earlier. In the dressing room Goochy admits, 'I was ready to walk for the first one, but not the second,' and although the two decisions evened themselves out, no umpire should ever compensate for an earlier decision. Cricketers have to concentrate on the next delivery and so should the umpire.

When they bat, Wood is dropped in the slips by Brears before he'd scored. If he'd caught that, I reckon Wood might've been on his way out of the side. He'd already angered the Australian Board by signing an option contract with Packer to play for WSC next year and a nought today would've meant four successive failures and a good excuse to drop him. Perhaps he'll get some runs tomorrow and make his position secure for at least this series.

Fifth day

We thought it would be hard work to bowl them out, but excellent bowling does the trick. We get the luck of some favourable umpiring decisions as well – especially when Wood's given out caught by myself. JK had bowled one at him outside the off-stump, he clearly heard something because he was up appealing right away. Tom Brooks took an age to lift his finger – JK was walking back – and Wood couldn't believe it either. Neither could I, but what could I do? Wood didn't play very well – he was dropped twice more today, each time by Boycs from mishit hooks off Both's bowling. Cosier played a clown of an innings – he got 47 but instead of trying to save the game for his side, he slogs all round the place like a Sunday League batsman. Not an impressive effort from the vice-captain. Toohey may have been unlucky to be given out – he clearly thought he didn't snick the ball to me from Hendo and I feel he may have been right.

Things got on top of Tom Brooks in this match and he announced his retirement at lunchtime. But you don't become a bad umpire overnight and it was just a bad match. But Wood didn't let him forget it and slammed him in a radio interview afterwards.

So we're two-up and we celebrate with champers again. More good news – the air strike is over and we can fly on to Adelaide as planned for the next stage of the tour. My immediate plans will be nothing more strenuous than resting my groin, but I manage to record an interview with the BBC's Chris Martin-Jenkins, wishing my family and friends happy Christmas. It'll be played on the radio a couple of days before Christmas Day and I appreciated the chance to give them all my love and best wishes . . .

GOWER The thunderstorm of the night before virtually killed off Aussie's chances and only Wood and Cosier – both using up a fair slice of luck – gave them hope. It's true we had more luck than them in this Test, but we had the greater teamwork, with our fielders far better at supporting the bowlers and trying to make things happen, rather than waiting for them to happen.

I rated Tom Brooks for the way he tried to change things when he returned to Australia after his year in English county cricket in 1977. In Aussie, there's a strong 'not out' tradition whenever the batsman's on the front foot, trying to lap or sweep the off-spinner. This is because it's thought the ball would have a long way to travel and could deviate from the stumps and also because the extra bounce might mean it would pass over the top. So for years English off-spinners, used to getting these decisions in England, have been blunted in Australia because the batsmen know they won't be given out LBW.

I've got no time for Wood's outburst against Brooks. Surely as a professional one must abide at all times by the umpire's decision. There are always times when it goes in your favour to help make up for the times when one feels aggrieved. I can think of times I have felt 'done' and it's been impossible to hide an immediate reaction, but to state obvious dissent after the game's ended cannot be good for anyone.

Second Test reflections

TAYLOR   We could have lost both of these first two Tests but our application pulled us through. Playing professional cricket seven days a week helps, because that means we're going to face more crises than these young Australians and learn to react accordingly. Our seam bowling strength was decisive – Hendo, Goose, JK and Both are a handy quartet when the wicket's helping them – and although we were justified in playing only one spinner, Dusty again bowled his off-breaks well. The away-swinger he trapped Cosier with was a beauty (my mind went back to the game against Western Australia four years ago when Fred Titmus had appeals for similar situations turned down time and again). Dusty picked up some useful runs as well and it's nice to see him chirpier and more confident.

I still think Higgs should have played for the Aussies. We just don't see his type of bowling in the county game. It doesn't matter if he's not as good a bat as Yardley – his job is to get wickets.

Overall a very satisfying team effort considering we were 3 for 2 on that first morning. It's nice to see Lulu take a Test attack apart, and it looks as if Boycs might be on the way back. My only worry at the moment is my groin injury – but at least I'm in good hands . . .

GOWER   I'm pleased for myself and for the team. I've realized one ambition with the bat and the team spirit is excellent. I'm still learning the importance of concentration but with Boycs at the other end when batting, and blokes like Chat in the field, not much is being missed. Our bowlers are all doing their bit and most of the worries are with the Aussies. But there's still a nagging doubt that either Test might have gone the other way. Higgs, with his tight control and bounce, should have played and the selectors seem to agree, because they've brought him back for the next Test. Cosier's dropped – not a great surprise, he hadn't looked too special and they've brought in Alan Border from New South Wales – he looked quite a good batsman in the State game against us in November.

One final reflection on Perth – it's been fun rooming with Henri. I like his arrogance, the way he takes an opposite stance with people at social functions and tests out his outlandish theories just for the fun of it all. He's a deep thinker and a good leg-puller.

MURPHY   England's professionalism, morale and teamwork were justifiably lauded, even in the Australian papers, but they took some brickbats for their scoring rate in the Perth Test. While the players pointed out that the results were the important factors (and that if the roles had been reversed, the Australians would have been content with a slow-scoring but *successful* side), much was made of the dwindling crowd figures and the correlation with declining run rates. Brearley pointed out that groundsmen should crop the lush outfields in Australia because this meant many shots weren't going to the boundary. The captain estimated that a quarter of the possible runs were being lost due to lush outfields but many felt that Boycott's presence in the side was the greatest inhibiting factor in run-rate considerations. Much was made of his first innings of 77 in 449 minutes with not one boundary – but its value to the side just couldn't be assessed in simple terms. It was an innings for the side as much as for himself, something that isn't often said about the Yorkshireman's efforts. His influence on Gower was also incalculable. The young left-hander was looking a class player, now that the confidence engendered from his helmet was banishing the early tour doubts. His off-side play in his century had old-timers recalling Frank Woolley and there were no longer any doubts over his quality or Test temperament.

There was a gulf in this match between both sides' fielding – a gulf that got wider as the tour progressed. In the next Test, Emburey came in and took over the gully position from Gower, leaving Gower to dominate one side of the field in the same way as Randall. With Taylor – despite his injury – characteristically immaculate, the Australians' efforts were sloppy in comparison, despite good individual efforts. Maclean had a poor match – Miller got him twice for an aggregate of one run and he didn't take Yardley's off-spin too confidently. Time was running out on the experienced Maclean, although his value to the young Australians couldn't be underestimated.

It was a significant match for Miller – with 65 runs and six wickets, he no longer had to worry about his place in the side. His first innings forty was particularly impressive and he ended the series with more wickets than any other off-spinner in Tests in Australia.

Hogg again bowled superbly – and he sent down 47 overs, helping to kill the asthma bogey still further. After just two Tests, he looked a class performer – straight, hostile, with the ability to move the ball away to supplement his usual off-cutters.

The umpiring that caused such controversy in this Test continued to be a problem throughout the series. Wood apologized for his outburst a few days later but the damage had been done. Both sides, anxious not to miss out, continued to vie with each other in the number of appeals in each session and before long the players' confidence in the umpiring was not high.

Once more England seemed to have selected wisely – Lever did his job well, taking the wickets of Wood in each innings and mopping up the tail on the final day. Old wasn't missed and his decision to drop out proved a grave error; he never played a significant part in proceedings for the rest of the tour. Edmonds, too, had to be content with twelfth-man duties.

In the end one of the crucial differences between the sides so far was that the Australians never really recovered after bad starts whereas England seemed to be able to claw back. So far the Australians hadn't managed more than eight for the first wicket – in the next Test that was rectified with appropriate results. England, on the other hand, continued to struggle at the start of their innings, but there always seemed to be someone on hand to breathe life into the flagging corpse at crucial times.

5

Adelaide and Melbourne
– Christmas

December 20

GOWER Given the South Australia game off, not too worried. Weather not very pleasant – warm and humid, overall lethargic air about the match. Manage to fit in a few games of tennis; Goochy comes closer to emulating John Newcombe than me, perhaps the moustache helped! Have a game with some locals and maintain England's ascendancy off the field by winning 6/3, 6/3 in the doubles.

Have some fun as the drinks waiter in the match. I wear the helmet on the first day (braving the crowds?) and then borrowed an umbrella from a lady. Tried to find a Santa Claus outfit, but no luck! The gestures were appreciated by the crowd because until the last innings the cricket seemed pointless. A good declaration by Bob Blewett sets us a reasonable challenge – 239 in 180 minutes and with some fine batting from Zap, Arkle and Dusty, we finish up with the scores level and our last pair together.

An interesting bloke bats number 11 for us – Boycs. To the amusement of everyone in the dressing room, Brears continues to leave him further down the list as the wickets fell. He hadn't been too impressive in the first knock (four runs in 90 mins) and he seemed to take it all in good spirit – 'I usually have to go out with some other bugger and come back by mysen, but this time I'm going out by mysen and coming back with someone.'

Lunch on the final day found us all in good humour – almost a trial run for Christmas lunch the next day. Highlight was JK's impersonation of the manager eating an orange. Doug always takes off the top of the orange and slurps his way through the rest –

so JK proceeded to decimate his, with orange peel, pips and segments exploding all over the place!

During the spell in Adelaide, myself, Chat, Embers and Arkle attend the local Cricket Society's meeting. Chat and I were booked to speak – I penned my thoughts in the car on the way and as usual the thought of speaking was worse than the business. I talked about the various cricket trips I'd had – to Ceylon, West Indies and Perth and threw in a few appropriate accents for good measure. One swear word as well by mistake, but all went well. E. W. Swanton also spoke and described my effort as 'verbal pyrotechnics', which I take to be a compliment! After that, a question-and-answer session to round off a pleasant evening – and it was nice to be thanked at the ground during play by several Society members . . .

TAYLOR   Still worried about my groin injury, although Bernie's doing his best to keep me cheerful. At my age I have to strive to play in every Test and Bernie says I'll be ninety-per-cent fit for next week's third Test. Brears asks me if I want a second opinion, I tell him there's no need and Brears says that he wants me to play even if I'm only ninety per cent. We knew the ball would keep low at Melbourne, following our match against Victoria in November, so it was nice to feel needed.

Chilly's in bed with migraine – poor bloke, if it's not one thing it's another. I visited him a couple of times. His room was darkened and he wasn't feeling too clever.

Christmas Eve

Fly to Melbourne and arrive in the worst storm I've ever seen. The wind was blowing, it was a bumpy landing and the lightning made it seem like daytime. Poor old JK wasn't happy in the plane, nor were the rest of us! We all sang carols in the coach to the hotel – under the leadership of you've guessed it . . . Arkle, standing up at the front of the coach doing his Malcolm Sargent bit.

Hendo and I went to midnight mass feeling a little sorry for ourselves because our cards from our wives hadn't arrived. There *were* others, of course, but there's no substitute for one from the wife, especially as we knew both had been posted. It was particularly hard on Hendo, because this has happened to him several times on tours. There'd been postal problems in Australia, but at the time – my sixth Christmas away from home in the last eight years – it seems no excuse. My worst night of the tour – it's pouring rain, I'm limping to mass with my bad groin, Hendo's down in the dumps, I've had no card from Cathy, and my daughter Claire's got chickenpox. Happy Xmas.

Christmas Day

A better day, some good fun. We have the traditional drinks with the British press at midday, then the team have lunch in fancy dress. The entertainments committee (Dusty and JK) had given each player a letter of the alphabet and we had to dress in clothes or as a character beginning with that letter. Both is a gorilla (how appropriate), Rad an Indian squaw, I'm an earl and Boycs comes with a white towel pinned underneath and a band over his head – none of us can work out what he's supposed to be. I hired my gear from the Adelaide Festival Theatre's costume department and I'm resplendent in wig, tailed coat, buckled shoes and tights.

After lunch, Dusty and Hendo give us their Derbyshire tap-room impressions. Dusty looks terrific – he's got a suit on belonging to the *Daily Mail*'s cricket writer, Alex Bannister, a cloth cap, white shirt without a collar, a red and white spotted hankie, a belt stuffed inside his trousers to give him a pot belly, the manager's brogue shoes and a fag sticking out of the side of his mouth. He and Hendo come out with great remarks like 'Who's this here Eddie Baslow who's captain of Derbysheer?' and 'This young David Gover looks a good bat' and 'That Spike Hendrome's bowling well for England.' Very good value.

Then it's Goose's turn, with some great impersonations of the radio commentaries we used to listen to years ago when the MCC were in Australia – he'd give us all the crackling and hissing from the radio with the occasional work coming through – 'And it's Miller to (crackle, crackle) . . . and (hiss, hiss) is . . . So the score's (crackle, crackle) for (hiss, hiss) . . .'

Goose's fancy dress was also a star turn. He was an Aussie umpire with white stockinet over his face to preserve his identity, dark glasses, a white stick and his finger kept going up all the time. On one of his pockets he had a huge badge saying 'Fiery's Favourite'. That went down well, even with Boycs, who's had a few words to say about Aussie umpires in his time!

Then Arkle used Goose's white stick to good effect, conducting a boys' choir which came to sing us carols. After that it's time to sleep it off or, in my case, have a sauna. I get through to Cathy on the phone twice, and the pouring rain helps me think of home. An enjoyable day which again showed our good team spirit, but I'm glad it's over.

GOWER   Embers and I ran the bar for the booze-up with the press. The fancy dress was a laugh – I emerge as the Chicago Kid, an apology for a cowboy with boots, stetson, but underneath a Chicago Pizza Parlour tee shirt – origins just off Pall Mall!

My room-mate Goochy becomes 'Zorro', very realistic but for a heavy wooden sword, manufactured at a moment's notice by the Adelaide groundsman. Arkle's Queen reflected some hard work and the manager's Inspector Clouseau was immaculate, including the French accent and the joke-shop moustache. He also penned a poem for Goose to recite, full of sharp witty references to people in the side and their characteristics. Very good value is the manager.

A version of the 'Twelve Days of Christmas' went down well. It was sung with individual lines (many unprintable) reflecting each person's characteristics or pet sayings – for example, when it was Kenny Barrington's turn it just had to be 'eleven bleedin' knockouts', a reference to his favourite phrase 'it's a bleedin' knockout'.

A good, light-hearted atmosphere, although tomorrow's one-day International isn't totally overlooked, even though the pouring rain lessens the prospects of it ever starting. Later on, myself, Rad and Zorro spend a few hours with Embers and his fiancée at her flat. Susie keeps pouring the wine and producing more food, so that the key to the evening is sleeping it off. Cabaret is provided by Julian, an uninvited guest. Despite two hours of leg-pulling, abuse and strong hints, he won't go until everyone disappears in the next room, leaving him on his own!

Boxing Day
No play because of rain, we didn't even have to go to the ground. In the afternoon, the weather clears up and myself, Chilly, Tolly, Both and Zap head for the Royal Melbourne Golf Club. Pleasant afternoon, perfect for cricket – shame about my form with the clubs.

TAYLOR I felt sorry for the Australian Board, because this was to be a big money-spinner for them. It's been re-arranged for February, but the big crowd would have been today's. More treatment from Bernie and spend some time in the sauna – still no real improvement in the groin. Have drinks with a few of the tennis players who are in the Australian Open – there's Tony Roche, Ken Rosewall, Ross Case, Arthur Ashe and Sue Barker. There's also the blond-haired golfer, Greg Norman, who seems very keen on Sue.

December 29
Still very wet, so little chance of practising in nets. Did some light training, although Brears had a net and gets six stitches put in his eye after being hit by a lifting delivery. He's okay and will open the innings in tomorrow's Test with Goochy dropping down to number four. We thought Gooch's strokeplay would be more useful down the order, while Brears and Boycs could hopefully see off the threat of Hogg and Hurst.

Embers also plays. He'd bowled well at Adelaide just before Christmas, he played grade cricket in Melbourne last season and so has experience of these wickets and with four left-handers in the Aussie side, plus Maclean's vulnerability against off-spin, it seemed sensible to play two of them.

I'm still not completely fit, but Bernie says I'll be all right. I feel I have to play because the wicket looks dodgy. There's no grass on the square itself, it's been badly treated with grass cuttings rolled onto the track. So it'll crack open when it dries out and the ball will keep low. It'll be a test of my wicket-keeping ability.

GOWER When I saw Brears with his swollen eye and the stitches, I said, 'Now you know how I feel every morning!' It was a good idea for Zap to go in number four, provided the openers could see off Hogg and co. There'd been some talk of Tolly getting into the side but I couldn't really see where. It couldn't be in place of Chat, so it had to be as a batter. He wouldn't be replacing any of the first six as far as I could see, so one of the two off-spinners would have to make way for him and that wouldn't be right in my opinion because both were bowling well. The make-up of the side seemed to be against Tolly, well though he's played whenever he's had the opportunity.

Melbourne is expected to be a good easy-paced wicket, but so far the wickets have all been variable. They've been doing more off the seam than the usual Aussie ones and although they are still bouncier and faster than in England, they haven't yet been as fast as their reputation.

There's a lot of talk at the moment about the poor crowds at the Tests and the need for a big attendance in this Test. As players we don't feel guilty about the comparatively poor turn-outs but from a selfish point of view we play better in front of a big crowd. They bring their own atmosphere and you respond accordingly. That's why it's easier to fire yourself in Test cricket than in a normal county match.

6
Third and Fourth Tests

Third Test, first day

TAYLOR Wood gets an unbeaten hundred. A rather lucky one; he played some streaky shots, his running between the wickets was unbelievable and if I'd been fit he would have been run out early on. The ball was pushed to Randall in the covers and Arkle hesitated till I could get up to the wicket with Wood stranded. When he saw I wasn't going to make it, he had a shy and missed, with Wood still out of his ground.

I caught Hughes for a duck off Both and although he thought it had hit his boot, I thought it was a straightforward edge. Then Hendo came up with a magnificent slip catch to get Yallop. He's the best slip catcher among pace bowlers that I've seen – his mental strength must be quite something, because he must be shattered after bowling an eight-ball over and then having to concentrate for the next over, instead of taking it easy down at long-leg.

Toohey again showed his weaknesses. He tends to play off-side shots with a braced left leg instead of bending it. This means he'll be playing in the air. He also has a habit of slogging the off-spin in the mid-wicket area and this is how he was dismissed, with Arkle diving forward to scoop up a mishit.

Border impressed me on his debut. I'd played against him four years ago and he looked a good player with a sound temperament even then. Brears crowded him when he came in near the end, but he stuck it out well. We must get him and Wood out quickly tomorrow.

Slightly disappointed at the end of the day. They rode their luck but we thought we might have winkled a few more out. If we'd batted, I think we'd have grafted better and put ourselves in an invincible position.

GOWER   At close of play, Brears suggests we hadn't looked as sharp as in the first two Tests; perhaps a degree of complacency had crept in, or a side-effect of Christmas. Certainly a few run-out chances went begging and two or three catches were spilled. Brears himself dropped a couple at slip and felt obliged to head for the outfield, even to the spinners, off whom he's held some good catches recently. Personally I felt quite fit on the chase, though not at my best when cutting the ball off at cover and mid-wicket. Perhaps I lack match practice in that area, having been at gully for most of the previous Tests – with Embers in his specialist gully position today, I'm back in the covers. It's amazing how one develops a rhythm in a fielding position. This applies very much to one's judgement or instinct in diving on the ball.

At the end of the day, there's a feeling that the Aussie batsmen are at last going to do themselves justice and give us a total to aim at.

Second day

TAYLOR   We're chuffed to bits to get them out so cheaply in the morning. Border's out in the first over and we bowl and field well, but many of them throw their wickets away, and their tail again looks a long one. Morale's sky high again, but Hogg gets Brears and Boycs out in one over. Watching Boycs being bowled on the TV playback, I'm amazed to see his right leg moving back to square-leg before coming back in line. I'd never seen him do that before and he couldn't believe it when I told him. He was getting square on and in no position to play the ball that was leaving him.

The pitch is deteriorating with a few shooters flying about. I'm bowled with one that comes ankle height, Lulu gets one that keeps low and the one that bowled Embers goes under his bat. Arkle gets in trouble with Doug Insole for staying at the crease when he was given out LBW and showing his bat to everyone because he thought he'd played the ball. Insole says: 'When you're given out, get off straight away.' Randall: 'I hit it, I hit it!' Insole: 'That doesn't matter, you've been given out – don't let it happen again' – and quite right too.

Dusty plays the slowest innings in Test cricket – 3 in 110 minutes; but there wasn't much leg-pulling in the dressing room about it. We all felt sick for our bowlers and in any case, Dusty did well to hang on.

That evening we attend another Perkins reception. Someone asks the increasingly hirsute Willis when he's going to get his hair cut. Bearing in mind that most Aussie barbers cut hair like sheep shearers, Goose's remark that he didn't fancy 'being dipped' before the shearing went down very well!

GOWER   After we'd hustled out the Aussies in the morning, Brears said, 'Well done, lads, now let's bat properly' – which we didn't! In the morning session, it looked a good, flat wicket but it cracked up quickly. The one that got me LBW kept a little low and it nipped back slightly into me. Game, set and match to Dymock – pity, really, I thought I'd played well and my 29 ended up top score!

The roar of the crowd when Hoggy bowled Boycs was amazing. I was downstairs, acting out a superstition because I thought I'd bring the openers luck by not watching the first few overs. But the noise was phenomenal and it makes me wonder what the atmosphere must have been like during the Melbourne Centenary Test with Lillee on song.

New Year's Eve

TAYLOR   The authorities have decreed this should be the rest day, because they want a big crowd tomorrow on the public holiday. More treatment and sauna sessions, reasonably happy with the injury and pleased with my keeping so far in the match. Saw in 1979 in the manager's room with Chilly, Dusty, JK and Lulu (wearing Guy's gorilla uniform!). Watched the Scottish country dancing on the telly, had one or two drinks and then to bed soon after midnight. A sleepless night; the Aussies have a habit of celebrating by tooting their car horns and I just happen to have a room overlooking the main road. And a Happy New Year to you, too . . .

GOWER   Early in the evening have a few drinks with some of the tennis players who are in the Australian Open. Interesting chat with one John Thirsk, who's John Newcombe's promotion manager. Talking to the players on the circuit and to John gives me further interest in the sport. Those average players who can't afford to pick and choose tournaments must spend a lot of time away from home, putting our four months in the shade. Mind you, they *do* have a certain control over their travels, whereas there's no way we can pop off home for a couple of weeks in mid-tour. On the whole, I prefer our sport, because you've got built-in friends in a touring party, whereas tennis is essentially a selfish game, which must surely harden up your temperament.

Not too keen on a rest day after just two days. I'm used to three straight days' cricket and then a rest, so I think, 'Just two days to go, I'm over the hump.' I know that makes Test cricket sound a bit of a job and on occasions it is, but that probably won't always be my attitude.

New Year's Day

TAYLOR   Good to get back in the game after kicking our heels yesterday. On a wicket that's cracking up even more, we give a good professional performance to have them 163 for 7 at the close. They didn't help themselves, though – again Kim Hughes showed his lack of concentration when he hit the first ball after lunch, a wide one from Both, straight to Lulu. He simply gave the bowler the charge when he should've been capitalizing on his excellent display before lunch.

Both was under instructions from Brears to unsettle Hogg as soon as he came in. Both fancies batting against bouncers, so he wasn't worried about Hoggy's retaliation. Hoggy doesn't like the short-pitched stuff and sure enough, he was bowled by Both fairly swiftly while anticipating a bouncer.

Must get the remaining three Aussie wickets early tomorrow because their lead is 278 and that will take a lot of getting on this wicket.

GOWER   Everything's sharper about our performance and Hendo epitomizes it with a superb back flick at short-leg to run out Border. That's the kind of effort that really gives the fielding side a boost and we did well for the rest of the day.

I'm enjoying the Melbourne crowd more than the others. Despite the usual quota of animals, they seem goodnatured generally. During a short stay at long-on I'm pleasantly refreshed by an anonymous yellow liquid. Each quaff by Yours Truly is met by cheers from the crowd and a chant later on of 'Gower is a piss-pot.' You can't win . . .

Off the field the pizza parlour takes a hammering from Goose, Rad, Dusty, Zap and myself. Two and a half dollars a head plus rough red wine give good value. Over the meal, Packer is discussed and we wonder if the English players who signed regret it. Apparently Derek Underwood watches our Tests very intently. Mind you, they made the decision and I suppose must take the consequences, however much anyone might sympathize.

Fourth day

TAYLOR We accomplish the first objective by getting their last three wickets for just four runs. So we need 282, the highest total in the game. We all know we must play forward whenever possible, although when Kenny Barrington says this, Boycs chimes in, 'How can you play forward against Hoggy when he pitches it short?' An odd comment from such an experienced player because obviously you don't play forward before the ball's released. But if it's well up, you mustn't play back because it'll skid through.

Disaster strikes early – Brears out for a duck. So frustrating, because he'd been batting well earlier in the tour. It was clearly getting him down but Rad's decline and Gooch's poor form was preventing it becoming a major problem. Arkle was LBW to a shooter, Goochy plays very well but gets a dodgy LBW at a crucial time. Both and Lulu give us hope for a time, but Higgs gets Both with a perfect leg-spinner and Lulu is LBW to one that kept low and should have been played off the front foot. Lulu takes it philosophically – like Goochy, he never complains when he gets back to the dressing room.

At the close we've got two wickets left and no hope. We'd known all along there wasn't much to choose between the two sides and this is the day that proved it.

GOWER Goochy played particularly well. Because the wicket was slow, he had plenty of time to go forward, and whenever Hoggy pitched one short he had time enough to play it down in front of his face. But an interesting LBW stuffs him and although Both and I thought we might get near the total during our partnership, it was not to be. I played a bit more like I do in England, trying not to be obsessive about going forward but leaning into the shot a little more. I still tried to keep that split second spare for any late adjustments off the back foot. I thought I played well until the second of two LBW appeals did me. I was apprehensive about the first one and I was given out next ball – LBW Dymock twice in the match!

The last half-hour was the crucial period – Both, myself, Dusty and Chat all went, while adding just eight runs. There was always the possibility that we might have sneaked near 283, but when you lose four wickets so quickly in the middle of the order, there's no chance.

Fifth day

TAYLOR   Nice to see 8,000 people turn up for a game that could have been all over in two balls! Brears was calm and sensible afterwards; he didn't say much, I could tell he was worried about his own form. This Test proved the Aussies were a better side than some of their supporters realized, although our side had to laugh when Yallop stood up at the presentations and told the crowd 'we can do it, we can do it'.

After the game I was interviewed for local TV with Hoggy and he impressed me with his down-to-earth comments. Everyone was going wild about him, saying what a great bowler he was, but he simply said, 'I might get nought for a hundred next Test.' It was the first time I'd had a long, serious conversation with him and I found him sensible and philosophical.

Looking back on this Test, I'm sure the toss was a crucial factor. I'd have fancied our bowlers against them in the fourth innings. But they took their chances and remembering Wood's complaints about the umpiring at Perth, it was interesting to note that seven LBW decisions were given against us and none against the Aussies. So we considered the slate wiped clean. It's funny how things even themselves out in cricket . . .

Disappointed but not down-hearted, I take an early flight to Sydney with Bernie so I can have extra treatment. It's still not a hundred per cent and towards the end of the match, it flared up again and got very sore. Still I was pleased with my keeping on a shooters' wicket – only four byes and *they* shot along the deck!

GOWER No immediate need for panic, although we're not totally unconcerned. We jested to the Aussie players that we only let them win to keep the series open! We'd felt all along there was little really wrong with their team, although the parts seemed more impressive than the whole.

Hoggy again was the star – I have a high regard for him and all these wickets he keeps getting can't just be down to luck or bad batting. He bowls nasty and straight, with a lot of off-cutters, though he can also swing it away from the bat, as Goochy found out at Perth. I've been lucky so far in that I haven't batted for very long against him, he often seems to be resting when I come in.

Dymock also bowled well and Higgs was economical. He also troubled Both, getting him in both innings.

I enjoyed the atmosphere, it really felt like a Test match. Pity the result wasn't right. *C'est la vie . . .*

MURPHY 'The Ashes Come Alight,' screamed the newspapers, and although such optimism seemed justified at the time, it proved a false dawn. England regained their grip on the series with professional out-cricket, astute leadership and gallant individual efforts at the right time. It seemed that the result was the best possible answer to the increasingly popular World Series Cricket, but as England tightened their grip on the series, the disillusioned Australian spectators showed what they thought of an unsuccessful national side.

The main worry for England concerned the form of the captain and vice-captain. It had been a long time since Willis had taken no wickets in a Test. His run-up was shaky, his feet still seemed to be troubling him and to make matters worse a virus laid him low in the next Test at Sydney. Already at this stage of the tour, his best performances were behind him – at Brisbane and Perth.

Brearley, with 37 runs in six innings in the series, faced the calls for his sacking with his usual equanimity. His team were still solidly behind him, still maintaining he was worth his place in the side for his captaincy alone – but there was no doubt they had their collective fingers crossed when he batted in the next Test.

His half-century in that match did much to cement his position, as did his dressing-room rocket given to the players at the end of the first day's play at Sydney. By the end of the tour, any worries about Brearley's batting capabilities were as much history as Yallop's grandiose claims of an Australian recovery in those first few days of January.

The toss, of course, was crucial but so was England's total of two and one for the first wicket. Australia put on over fifty for the first wicket in each innings and in the end that margin separated the sides.

The fact remained that the Australian tail was a long one – in the first innings, their last six wickets added eleven runs and in the second, the last five put on just fifteen. They never solved their lack of a Test class all-rounder, while England – with two in Botham and Miller – continued to sell their wickets dearly throughout the series, proving that when there's little to choose in terms of natural ability, the side with the greater application and morale usually wins.

January 4

GOWER Sydney's a nice spot, especially near the Harbour and the Opera House. The bridge is an imposing sight and there are some fine views in the area. After training and nets in the afternoon, Bernie, Chat, Dusty, JK and myself head for a small beach. Not highly recommended, but it's set in one of Sydney's better areas. Some beautiful properties, suitably decorated with Rolls-Royces, Mercedes and other appropriate knick-knacks.

Later a reception with the Governor, Lord and Lady Cutler, at Government House, a beautiful old mansion. Harold Larwood is there and one notable quote emerges when it is suggested to him that the travelling must've been the worst part of touring. Came the reply, 'No, the cricket.'

Certainly travelling's much smoother nowadays. So far on this trip there have been virtually no cock-ups – just one plane delayed for more than an hour and a bus that arrived half an hour late. But the cricket never seems to stop, especially just now with two Tests and a one-day International in the first fortnight of 1979.

January 6

TAYLOR   A big press and TV build-up for tomorrow's first day of the Fourth Test. Yallop's saying to every journalist who will listen, 'We can do it, we can do it – we can beat them 4/2.' He's getting our backs up with his forecasts and we still fancy ourselves with the pressure on. We've got much more experience of tight corners *and* a better captain.

If you look at the make-up of both sides, we're ahead in two vital departments – if we get through their first five batsmen they're in trouble and they also lack a fifth class bowler. Border will bowl his left-arm spinners if necessary but he hasn't the class to bother Test batsmen.

We are worried about Goose, though. He says his feet are okay now, but his rhythm seems to have gone. He struggled in the last Test and in the nets today. He's always fairly quiet about his own problems and never shouts his mouth off about what he's going to do in the forthcoming match, but I worry that we ask too much of him in Tests. I know that he's concerned about the change in character in these Aussie wickets – they don't compare with the ones he bowled on in his two previous tours with England and he's hardly had one to suit him so far on this trip. This one at Sydney doesn't look as if it'll do Goose any favours. Kenny Barrington says it's the best he's seen so far and that he'd love to bat on it, but I'm not too sure. It looks over-used because of the demands of Packer cricket on the Sydney cricket ground and I don't expect it to last five days. I can see our spinners doing well on it, so the toss is a vital one to win.

Still worried about my groin, although Bernie says one of these days it'll all come good. Hope that day arrives soon . . .

GOWER   Not much to discuss at the pre-Test team meeting and afterwards, Goose, Chat and myself test out a little Italian restaurant just down the road. Pizza very filling and the basic claret washes things down very well – just the job, helps calm those anxieties for a while.

An interesting chat with Boycs. He said I always appeared calm and unruffled. I told him it's an impression I like to give, especially if people are panicking all over the place. But I tell him

I have a few twinges of nerves now and again. I get on well with Fiery – he calls me 'Star' and 'Slogger' – and I enjoy the talk. It made me think that one acquires nerves the more one plays. My theory is that you play without worries at the start of your career but, as the pressures build up, so do the little tensions and from there it's a question of character to subdue them. Everything is mostly relieved when batting, it's the preconceptions of what might happen that are the worst.

For the rest of the time my easygoing feeling takes over and that's essential for relaxation. One can't afford to take the tensions of the game outside the ground. I like to forget these tensions in the evening, though some discussion doesn't go amiss and there's also the duty not to forget tomorrow's job.

Fourth Test, first day

TAYLOR   At last Brears wins the toss and we proceed to mess it up – all out 152, Australia 56 for 1. Both saves us with a typically swashbuckling fifty and Hendo and Goose help him add 54 to show the rest of us up. Arkle is out second ball, hooking it straight to backward short-leg. He slumps in the dressing room, with his head in a towel, saying, 'I play that shot well, the hook gets me lots of runs, I'm in good form, so I tried it.' Kenny Barrington says, 'It doesn't matter how many runs you've picked up – you've got to look at the wicket for a few overs before trying the hook.' Arkle: 'But I play that shot well.' Barrington: 'Not to the second ball!'

Goochy gets himself out; he'd been playing well, when he hits a long-hop from Higgs to the only man deep on the legside. It was a good catch but why the hell didn't he do what we're instructed as schoolboys – and hit the ball *down*? We didn't need to say anything to him in the dressing room, he knew what he'd done wrong.

The heat is intense and Goose, Hogg and Maclean all have to go off – the keeper's suffering from the effects of drugs he had to take when he was hit over the eye at practice yesterday. By the look of him, he shouldn't have played but I'm only ninety-percent fit myself, so I can't say much.

We knew we had to bowl tightly when they went in but although Goose gets Wood in the first over, we were terrible. We bowled too many bouncers and Darling hooked us out of sight – he played the shot much better than in the State game against us. I thought, 'Bloody hell, we're coming a right cropper here, we've got to get a grip' – and by the reaction of some of the other lads, I wasn't alone in my thoughts.

At close of play, we're in the dressing room, feeling really down, wondering if the tide is turning against us. Hendo says to me, 'It's just like the times we've thrown it all away at Derbyshire – what we want now is a bloody good rollicking.' Luckily Brears overheard this, sent JK to round up the others and he gave us just that for half an hour. We all had to take it quietly because the bowlers and the batters had cocked it up equally today. 'I want 110 per cent effort tomorrow', says Brears and his voice was one of controlled anger. It was good captaincy in my opinion – another skipper might have let it ride, but I think he judged our mood just right. We wanted to be told we were rubbish and I can't wait to get at them tomorrow.

GOWER A bad day for us all. I was out, caught behind just before lunch. Hurst bowled one that followed me; I tried to drop the wrists, but I couldn't get out of the way and gloved it. Thank God for Both – it was good to see one of us take the game to them. He hooked Hogg very well but eventually got a top edge to him.

Having played under Ray Illingworth for some time and suffered some of his rockets, it was interesting to compare the one from Brears. Illy would have been more forceful ('You were bloody rubbish, it's back to the ABC of cricket for all of you') but Brears' quieter style was effective. 'Blasé' and 'depressed' were two of the words he used to describe our efforts – I feel the former is more relevant. Certainly some of the early tour enthusiasm has gone and with Hendo backing Brears up in more forceful tones, it was the right time to let us have it.

Second day

TAYLOR A great, wholehearted effort, with the temperature at one stage 103 degrees. Goose has to go back to the hotel – he's in a bad way, allegedly suffering from heat exhaustion but in fact it's a virus. Hendo has to go off at one stage suffering from the heat – he sits on a chair under a cool shower to recover, says he's never known heat like it. In the circumstances Both's determination and enthusiasm are tremendous – twenty-odd overs and two catches. We had our luck, with Hughes again throwing his wicket away to the first ball of Goose's spell just after lunch when he chased a wide one. Surprised the Aussies only scored 49 in the last session. Border was well set and he should have capitalized on our tired attack. Perhaps a touch of inexperience?

At the end of the day, they're 96 ahead with three wickets left. We're back in the game and we all felt we'd done a good day's work.

GOWER   Hendo bowled his guts out but Guy's aggression and courage were invaluable. He always wants to bowl, he's like an Australian in the way he loves to be in the action. I know Brears appreciates how much Both wants to bowl at any stage – and today he had plenty of opportunity for that.

Last night's set-to certainly seems to have worked. We stuck to the task well in trying conditions and at the end Brears said 'That's much better, well played.' The feeling is that we're well in contention again, especially if the wicket starts turning.

Third day

TAYLOR   They lead by 142 and, to add to our problems, Boycs is out LBW first ball to Hoggy's loosener! Character's needed to get out of this one now and, happily, Brears gets some runs at last. Arkle (desperately close to being LBW before he'd scored) adds over a hundred with him, before Brears is beaten by a good one from, of all people, Border. We're delighted for Brears and for ourselves of course. Kenny Barrington had been on at him to play straighter and it worked. In the end I think fatigue got to him.

The heat's bloody unbelievable – two drinks intervals every session and the fielders were sheltering under the WSC floodlight pylons to get some shade. One occasion when Kerry Packer's eyesores were of some use to established Test cricket!

Arkle stuck out magnificently, geeing himself up and we were willing him to stay in till the close. But Yallop's field placing helped him – poor old Higgs often only had one slip and Hogg invariably bowled to an off-spinner's field rather than that of a class opening bowler. I couldn't understand how he could be so defensive with such a big lead and although someone must have had a word with him at tea and got him to attack more in the last session, the damage was done. Still, who's complaining? . . .

Boycs has trouble with the crowd today; while he was fielding in front of the Hill, gherkins, oranges and eggs were thrown at him. I could hear the abuse hurled at him while I was keeping wicket ninety yards away and I suggested to Brears that we should rotate the fielders down that end. But Boycs would have none of it and stayed put. You've got to admire the man's guts.

In the evening some light relief. The team are invited to the opening night of Johnny Speight's *The Thoughts of Chairman Alf*, starring Warren Mitchell in a one-man show. Very funny and a welcome break from the tensions.

GOWER Both gave the crowd a taste of their own medicine when he bowled Dymock – a few gestures in the appropriate direction, etc. It's all very well for people to deplore such actions but they don't get the stick handed out by the yobs on the Hill. I wouldn't do what Both did, I'd try to rile them in a different, quieter way but it was amusing to see him get them going.

Everyone was genuinely delighted for Brears and considering the heat and the state of the game it was a great effort. He was annoyed with himself when he got out, but to be fair it was a good ball from Border.

The press and TV commentators are complaining about our slow scoring. What do they expect? The game's still only halfway over and we've just got to play and play and use up time as well as score runs. We're waiting for the wicket to deteriorate and we're trying to wear down the bowlers. It's all very well telling us to give the ball a belt but we'd be hammered by the media if we lost our wickets in a couple of hours by trying to score quick runs. We're playing the way we know best and Yallop and co. must be worried now . . . The struggle's on and I think it's a bloody good Test match . . .

MURPHY The struggle was on for England in more ways than one. With the heatwave sapping their energies – birds were dropping dead out of the sky and a TV cameraman fainted, fell off his scaffolding and fractured his shoulder blades – some of the players were feeling unwell. Taylor still wasn't fully fit, Willis was confined to his hotel room for nearly the rest of the match and then Gower went down with a throat infection . . .

Rest day

GOWER   After a quantity of wine last night, I expect to lie in for a while, but feel more dead than expected. I doze through the morning and, unusually, through the afternoon. Throat very sore. I summon Bernie and he tells me I've got a temperature of 102. Magic. My room-mate, Both, isn't particularly overjoyed. He was very tired, although we thought that was more due to his bowling exertions. Anyway we both take an early kip with the hopes that I would bat tomorrow. I didn't want to bother the rest of the team with it, so I kept cramming the tablets and antibiotics down the throat.

Fourth day

Not much better, throat still painful, temperature now only 101. Bernie tells me to take my time and get to the ground about a quarter of an hour before the start. Over a late breakfast, I chat with Scyld Berry about my feelings just before I go in to bat. I tell him it's not until practice is over (i.e. 10.15) that the adrenalin starts to pump. I don't like being next man in at the start of play because I never seem to play well in that first hour, my body doesn't seem to function too well. I prefer going in about half an hour before lunch, that gives me time to play myself in and possibly pick up a few runs from tiring bowlers.

Goochy is given out and I duly bat half an hour before lunch. Feel a little weary but glad to be involved and hit a few off-side shots. At lunch, I slump over a chair with my head in my arms and Goose quips, 'I see Lulu's feeling better then!' I'm out soon after to a careless waft of the magic wand – caught by the keeper. Annoyed with myself, felt I'd let the side down because I'd got through the worst.

Disappointed, I return to the hotel and take to my bed. I sleep for a while but feel the urge to see how the game's going and switch on the TV at four o'clock (in Aussie, the coverage starts at 11 am, except in the state where the Test is being played – crowd considerations mean that coverage doesn't start till four o'clock today). Arkle's still there and he eventually gets a highly creditable 150. Just right for the situation, even though the commentators are still moaning that we should've got runs quicker. The game's evenly balanced at the close – we lead by 162 with four wickets in hand – and we mustn't lose wickets too quickly tomorrow.

TAYLOR Lulu played very well for 100 minutes. He was out chasing a wide half-volley but nobody would criticize him because he's battled away so bravely.

Arkle's was a real character innings, a complete contrast to some of his recent knocks where he's given his wicket away playing rash shots. When he was given out LBW he was off like a shot – no doubt mindful of the rockets given to him by the manager for staying too long after the decision – but some of the crowd still booed him as he came in, whether it was for previous gestures by him or for his slow scoring I'm not sure. I pulled his leg afterwards because he's been saying for a few weeks that he was going to score a double hundred. I said, 'You failed today, didn't you?' and he smiled, 'I'll get it next time.' He's a funny lad: something seems to compel him to jump around, play to the crowd and live off his nerves. But he's a Test batsman and today he played a really professional innings.

Brears says if we can scrape together enough runs to lead by two hundred we're in with a chance because the wicket will turn. So Dusty and me – the not-out batsmen – have a job on our hands tomorrow.

Went to the opera in the evening with Brears and his parents. It was Benjamin Britten's *Albert Herring* and the Opera House was very impressive – space-age design and a siren instead of the usual curtain-call bell. Unfortunately Brears and I were so mentally shattered from watching Arkle's innings that we couldn't keep our eyes open and had to leave with one act to go, leaving Mr and Mrs Brearley to hail a taxi back to the hotel.

Fifth day

Dusty and I hold out for an hour and we set them 205 in 270 minutes. No mishaps before lunch, but afterwards Wood again gets into trouble with his calling and runs himself out – he hit one straight to Both and calls for a run! Our lucky day? Hendo bowls superbly, again gets the important breakthroughs and Dusty and Embers clean up on a turning wicket. MacLean again falls to Dusty. Brears sets a 7/2 field for the off-spinners with just mid-off and cover on the off-side, and Dusty and Embers bowl well to their field. The bat/pad catches come regularly and only Border shows any stomach for the fight by using his feet and employing the pull to good effect.

When Yallop comes in, I can't resist a dig at him. He had said in the press that morning that, unlike England, his side would play attacking cricket and if necessary go down fighting. 'Are you going to play attacking cricket, then?' I said and he just smiled. Within a few minutes Hendo caught and bowled him and they were right in it . . .

We win with 55 minutes to spare for one of the best wins in modern Tests. And we've retained the Ashes! A great win for Brears – he batted well, captained the side brilliantly and gave us a tongue-lashing just when it was needed.

MURPHY   While England tightened the screw on the Australians, not all of the victorious side were cheering on the victory from the dressing room . . .

GOWER   Still 'enfevered' and spared duties at the ground. Another addition to my minor ailments – plague-like swellings on my face! What it is to be ugly and deformed. Highly boring to be sat/lying in the chamber. Keep gargling salt water, downing glasses of salt tablets, and massaging the neck. Feel generally grotty; where is the cure-all wonder drug? What about a bionic throat, or do they rust?

Listen to music on the radio and switch on the cricket at four to be pleasantly amazed by the turn in fortunes. We stuff them and I wish I was in the dressing room at that moment! I rise from my bed to try to join in the celebrations but after one beer retire again. Brears, with the tensions gone, seems pleasantly relaxed but also elated – deservedly so.

One or two of our lads aren't perfectly sober by the end of the night, but I'm in bed feeling sorry for myself wondering how one beer can kill me off so quickly!

Fourth Test reflections

TAYLOR   Considering that first day, it was a great victory and if I was an Aussie, I'd be reflecting now on the importance of good captaincy. Brears shook the lethargy out of us at just the right time and got us in the mood to grind them down.

The Aussie press gave their lot a roasting but we didn't get much praise for our efforts. They seemed obsessed with our slow scoring, ignoring the fact that we had to bat cautiously to use up time as well as score runs. Some said Brears' tactics were playing into the hands of Packer, but I reckon the public would have settled for a *successful* Aussie captain and to hell with the scoring rate. No country likes its national side to win more than Australia. Not that there's been a lot of exotic strokeplay in the World Series games. In many of the Packer games I've so far seen or read about, the scoring's been slow with the bowlers on top. In my opinion, this match proved the supremacy of Test cricket – it had tight moments, bags of character and above all, a result, even if it took a long time to achieve it.

Our bowlers were magnificent – Hendo only picked up four wickets but plugged away superbly, beating the bat time and again. He's almost like Max Walker in the way that he never gets the wickets he deserves. His length is just a little short, so that the ball will bounce over the stumps if he beats the bat and sometimes the ball does too much and the delivery's too good for the batter to touch it. But he gets so many wickets for other bowlers with his nagging accuracy because the batsmen take chances down the other end – I know Both appreciates this fact.

Although I didn't get one victim in the match, I enjoyed keeping wicket. My groin injury seemed to get easier as the match went on and it was nice to stand up to the off-spinners for 79 overs.

I was pleased with my shoulder-high takes down the legside – one ball from Dusty pitched outside the off-stump and went over Kim Hughes's left shoulder to me on the legside!

Dusty and Embers contrasted each other nicely – Embers is three inches or so taller, so he can give it more flight and get more bounce. Mills pushes it through quicker and is more economical with a nice away-swinger. When they got the Aussies on a wicket that helped them on the final afternoon, they did their job very professionally.

The heat in this match was the worst I'd yet experienced in Australia – which makes our victory even more impressive. But at the end, I'm absolutely shattered– – we've had ten days of real pressure cricket with hardly a break and now all I want to do is relax and look forward to Cathy coming out in a week's time.

GOWER   Despite my illness, it was a great feeling to be part of a side that had retained the Ashes. A lot of players had been to Australia in sides that had been stuffed out of sight – Goose, Hendo and Chat for a start – and, at the age of twenty-one, I realize I'm lucky. What's even more pleasing is that our victory was achieved with a side that wasn't fully fit and after a disastrous first day. Much is being made in the press about that first-day rollicking from Brears. Many are calling it the turning point of the match – it wasn't, that came in our second-innings performance. Brears' comments marked the start of the recovery.

All the talk of slow scoring tended to obscure the merit of our performance. The end justifies the means for the Aussies just as it does for us and, if the positions had been reversed, Yallop would probably have tried to do the same – although his batsmen don't have our resilience and powers of concentration. Much was made of some uncharacteristically slow scoring by Both in the second knock (6 in 90 mins). What the critics didn't realize was that, at that stage, it was vital for Both to use up time. If he'd played his normal way, he might've got a quick twenty in thirty minutes and then got out. That extra hour was far more decisive than the 14 runs he didn't score.

MURPHY It was a fascinating, fluctuating Test, giving cogent proof that the scoring doesn't have to be high-speed stuff if the quality of the match is gripping enough. Despite the poor crowds (possibly due to the heat as much as the slow scoring) and the critical press comment, the Fourth Test contained all the essential ingredients – a great fight-back by a side hampered by illness, fine individual batting performances from Darling, Botham, Border and Brearley and a century full of character by Randall. And in an era dominated by seamers, it was pleasant to note that no fewer than 180 overs were bowled by the spinners. And the match also had a result, with the eventual winners in doubt until the last couple of hours' play.

Some crucial moments favoured England – the four catches dropped off Higgs in the second innings, Randall perilously close to being LBW as soon as he came in, Yallop's negative field placings, Wood running himself out with just 167 to win and all ten wickets in hand. But perhaps the most important moment came on the second day with the score 126 for 1 and Australia needing just 27 for the lead. Willis, almost out on his feet, bowled a loosener to Hughes in the first over after lunch, only for Hughes again to show a fatal lack of concentration by hitting it straight to cover. With Darling firing away at the other end, he and Hughes could have put the game beyond England's reach within a couple more hours.

In just a week, Brearley's position had become unchallenged. All the old doubts and forebodings were forgotten and the side progressed triumphantly to a crushing series victory. In objective terms, this splendid English win was the worst thing to happen to the series and the hopes harboured by many that World Series Cricket would get its come-uppance. Attendances at the four Tests were already 100,000 down on the 1974/5 tour, and interest declined further in the next month while the Packer style prospered. A sobering thought for those delegates from the International Cricket Conference who were in Australia at the time to discuss a possible compromise with WSC. The longer the series progressed, the more pressure was put on the ICC and the Australian Board to be the ones making the concessions.

7
Sydney – Newcastle – Tasmania – Melbourne – Adelaide

January 12

GOWER Out of bed at last but still not feeling too great. Temperature normal, so take a stroll down the Cross – past the prostitutes, snack bars, blue-movie cinemas, etc. and end up in a pub just off the edge of the area. Although it's a better than average looking alehouse, the clientele include the biggest collection of derelicts in Sydney. All shapes, none attractive, all ages, a fair range of race and colour – some 'abos', a couple of negroids, a few Aussies, none of them looking too clever. All have one thing in common – alcohol – and one or two of the younger ones apparently need other drugs as well to get high. Furthermore, there seemed to be a substitutes' bench in the park a hundred yards up the road, where the same old 'derros' would be sleeping off the first session and waiting to go back later.

The Club Cricket Conference is in town and they include some old friends of mine from the St Lawrence Club, a Kent League side I played for during my university career. They include John Kilbee and Richard Walker and another friend, Jeff Jones from Reading. We pass the time very pleasantly and among the conversational topics is helmets. I tell them that despite the diehard's view that people never used to need them, two clear instances of their wisdom occurred this week. In the Test, Both was saved from very serious injury when Darling pulled a ball onto his head at short-leg. Despite evasive action, he didn't have time to escape. Even *with* his helmet, he had a very sore bonce for some time. Then in a Packer match, the helmet of Kepler Wessels produced four leg-byes and saved a headache. My blow from Hogg in the Perth Test missed the helmet and hit my neck but I knew that protection wasn't far away. What the critics seem to ignore is that people have been struck on the head since the game began and that helmets are merely a sensible form of protecting the most vulnerable part of the body. I wager there are some bygone batsmen who, pride apart, might have been very glad of a helmet at some stage in their career.

January 13
Back to work for the one-day International. After eight overs the rain comes down and the game's over. Rather glad because although I declared myself fit, my co-ordination seemed less than perfect, as proved where the boot made contact with the ball instead of my hand when I was trying to stop an overthrow!

MURPHY The one-day Internationals seemed dogged by the weather in what was an exceptionally dry Australian summer. It was arranged to play the three matches in a ten-day period in a fortnight's time and the sponsors, Benson and Hedges, kept their fingers crossed. They were unlucky – only one of the matches was closely fought, the other two finished early because of batting collapses by either side.

The bulk of the team flew off to Newcastle to play an up-country game against Northern New South Wales. Staying behind in Sydney for a well-deserved rest were Willis, Hendrick, Botham and Taylor.

TAYLOR Hendo and I go down to Camp Cove, a little beach just out of Sydney. The beach is packed with topless girls, and it's a great strain to look at them! We both agree it looks better to see a girl wearing a bikini bra. The ones who take off their tops are only trying to attract attention to themselves and it's amazing how much respect one has for those who cover themselves up. Sounds old-fashioned I know, but it's true!

A headache next day for the manager and it's caused by Both and Goose. For the last forty-eight hours we haven't heard a thing from them and we're due to fly out to Tasmania in a few hours. At lunchtime, with Doug Insole desperate, they both stroll in, say they've been with friends, lazing around, eating and drinking and listening to some of the best hi-fi sounds in Australia! We were annoyed, particularly at Goose as vice-captain and he agreed he'd been wrong not to phone in.

GOWER   The Newcastle game was completely irrelevant, except for one player – Tolly. My poor old landlord fractured his cheek when he missed a straight one while batting. His injury adds spice to the helmet arguments. He doesn't look too good – swollen right cheek, eyes closed and blood oozing from a plaster on his cheek. Seems fairly philosophical and in good care.

I'm due to carry out the drinks, but because of Tolly's injury I have to do a fair bit of fielding. The atmosphere's completely dead, understandable after the exertions of the previous fortnight, but it's still very hard to fire oneself. Try to enjoy myself in the field and spend a fair bit of time checking out the crowd for crumpet.

Brears is in a light-hearted mood, giving Chilly a hard time for beating the bat three-quarters of the time during his first five overs. Kenny Barrington affords some amusement when he tells us the local cricket association are laying on a smorgasbord for us. 'Don't worry about the food tonight, lads,' he says, 'it's English – Smorgas Gas Board!'

The crowd seems to be eighty per cent kids, all keen autograph hunters. I spend most of the first day just signing, thought I might've done my bit, but no! Still going strong on the third day. Arkle spends one two-hour session just signing. Boycs does most of his on the field, he's constantly surrounded by about twenty kids during play. Perhaps their keenness stems from the lack of other attractions in Newcastle.

Some pleasant diversions – I meet up with Glamorgan's Allan Jones and Richard Williams from Northants, both former colleagues on the Young England tour to the West Indies in 1976. Ian Richards, also of Northants, is playing club cricket in this area. Jack Walsh, the former Leicestershire left-arm spinner, is also here. A good man, easy to talk to and not hung up in his own

On the plane trip from Perth to Adelaide, a game of cards passes the time for Gower, Randall, Miller and (partly hidden) Botham (*photo: Patrick Eagar*)

The first dip in the hotel pool at Adelaide for John Emburey and David Gower (*photo: Ron McKenzie/News Ltd, Sydney*)

To liven up the proceedings Gower wears batsman's protective headgear when he undertakes the dangerous job of serving drinks during the South Australia match just before Christmas (*photo: Ron McKenzie/News Ltd, Sydney*)

Taylor (the earl), Radley (the Indian squaw) and Gower (the Chicago Kid) head for the Christmas Day fancy dress party with suitable replenishments

Doug Insole in his starring role as Inspector Clouseau at the Christmas Day party. Geoff Boycott is on the left (*photo*: *Bernard Thomas*)

The England party in full fancy-dress regalia on Christmas Day: (left to right) Brearley, Lever, Boycott (standing), Edmonds, Gower, Geoffrey Saulez the scorer (partly hidden), Radley, Botham, Old (partly hidden), Gooch, Miller and Tolchard (both seated), Barrington, Emburey and Randall (both standing), Bernard Thomas the physiotherapist and, with his arm around him, Hendrick (*photo*: *Bernard Thomas*)

(Above) Melbourne prior to the third Test: (left to right) Botham, Gower, Edmonds, Brearley, Insole (partly hidden) and Barrington (*photo: Patrick Eagar*)

The Sydney Hill in session during the fourth Test (*photo: Patrick Eagar*)

era. He bowls a few at Tolly (pre-injury) for the benefit of the local TV cameras and it's interesting to see the old chinamen come out, we don't see a lot of them in the modern game. He still keeps in touch with people like Mike Turner at Leicester and he's keen to catch up on all the news. His wife's a Leicester girl and they're happy to talk about familiar places and faces they remember.

Fit in some roast beef, thank God, but spending the evenings in an alcoholically-orientated environment doesn't exactly help my convalescence.

Leaving Newcastle is not without frustration. Our bus driver takes it upon himself to give a commentary on places of alleged interest on the way to the airport – the workers' club, the factories, the office buildings, even a couple of holes in the bleedin' road. There's nothing of historical interest in Newcastle, compared even with the most basic English village – and it turns out that all the driver wanted was some autographs. Why didn't he ask and just leave the radio on? Feeling tired and hungry and it didn't help my mood. End up in Launceston sometime after midnight, absolutely knackered. Pick up the bags out of the rain and collapse a.s.a.p.!

MURPHY While the players prepared for their matches in Tasmania, the rumour machine in the press was working overtime. A Sydney newspaper linked Gower and Botham with World Series Cricket, but Gower categorically denied any involvement. 'I know nothing about it, I haven't been approached,' he said, 'and in any case, I'm very happy with the way things have gone with the England team and with the way I've been treated.' The press were also smacking their lips at the prospect of a meeting on the field between Boycott and the man taking over from him as Yorkshire's captain, John Hampshire – at present coaching in Tasmania and due to play twice against the tourists. Will they talk to each other? Who will make the first move? Will they smoke a pipe of peace? With the series won, these considerations seemed more important to the media at the time than any rational assessment of England's progress . . .

January 17

TAYLOR   We're allowed a rest day, so after some light training, eight of us play golf at the Launceston Club. I'm playing with Henri and on the first tee (a par four, 265 yards long) he hits a screamer to within a yard of the pin and sinks the putt for an eagle! The members' faces were a picture! A professional couldn't have hit that shot better . . .

In the evening a barbecue in a house owned by the President of the Tasmanian Cricket Association, Tom Roome – and what a house! It's like one of those rambling houses you associate with the deep south of America and then a swift walk past the tennis courts takes you into his son's house, which is equally magnificent – swimming pool, huge dining-room table made of maple, snooker table in the games room and an amazing hi-fi set. Mrs Radley and Mrs Gooch were with us and they were open-mouthed . . . And yet Tom's supposed to be a retired schoolmaster. How's he managed all this?

GOWER   Launceston's a delightful spot, very green (there's a lot more rain than in Australia) and the whole atmosphere's very therapeutic. Drive up with Arkle to Cataract Gorge, a local beauty spot only five minutes out of town. A pleasant spot, it's blessed with a swimming pool, a restaurant and a chair lift across the water in the centre of the gorge. Very English surroundings – stately home type gardens, including peacocks. Dusty, JK and Goose are already there. On the way back a quick look at the local pub. Again it's English in character – apart from the beer!

Highlight of the evening at the President's house is the powerful Sony stereo system. Nice loud freak-out to 'Saturday Night Fever', Neil Diamond and the Little River Band. Very relaxing because the lack of my own cassettes has deprived me of much pleasure. Any time I get near a music system is bliss to me and fatal to the owners!

January 18

TAYLOR   We play Tasmania in a limited-over match and beat them easily. They've just won the Australian Gillette Cup and their hero is their captain, Jack Simmons, the Lancashire all-rounder. He won the Final's Man of the Match award with four cheap wickets and an unbeaten half-century and it's nice to see him doing so well, he's a good bloke who's put a lot into the game.

In his speech after the game, Jack says today's defeat was the best thing to happen to his team because they now knew how to play limited-over cricket after watching us. He's the top man out here and when he told the Cricket Association he couldn't come back next year because he was organizing his benefit season back home, they were very upset. In fact, some businessmen have offered to cover him for the amount he's likely to make from his benefit, but Jack wouldn't do that, it's not fair to the Lancashire supporters.

One item on today's agenda was deferred. Jackie Hampshire couldn't play against us today because his son was hit on the head with a cricket ball and he had to take him to hospital. So the clash of the Yorkshire giants is delayed for twenty-four hours!

Next day the three-day game starts against Tasmania and Boycs and Hampers are within a yard of each other but don't speak! When the second wicket falls we were all gathered together round the wicket when we saw Hampers walking in. We were very interested to see if there'd be any reaction from either, but as Hampers drew near to the wicket, he appeared to brush past Boycs without saying anything and Boycs turned on his heel and walked away to mid-off.

Anyway, Hampers didn't last long – Chilly, who was bowling magnificently, had him caught by myself second ball with a superb outswinger. So, at the end of the day, Boycs was 41 not out, I was batting with him and he looked determined to get a hundred, perhaps to show Hampers who was the better bat . . .

'Bluey' Bairstow (God knows why he's called that) has been flown in to replace the injured Roger Tolchard and he marks his debut on the tour in strange circumstances. He fields instead of Dusty for five minutes, has a shy at the wicket and hits the umpire up the backside instead! Good start . . .

We're staying at an hotel with a casino, and Both proceeds to lose a hundred dollars in five minutes at roulette. The previous week he won eighty dollars at cards, he doesn't seem to care about money, but really loves life.

GOWER   When he came in to bat, Hampers said, 'Good mornin', how are you?' to Boycs, who didn't appear to take much notice. There was nobody else near Boycs so the greeting must've been directed at him. I found it all rather amusing, not that it's really got anything to do with any of us, apart from the Yorkshiremen in the party.

Boycs looks in good nick in the evening session. I get my usual sort of thirty-odd before smearing at my first ball from the leg-spinner and missing it. Zap, with a big smile on his face, described it as 'a shot for a day off tomorrow . . .'

Entertained by Hampers at his house, accompanied by 'Bluey' Bairstow – funnily enough, Boycs is nowhere in sight! The man in question is not even discussed.

The next day's play is affected by rain. During the morning, as we wait for it to ease off, the injury jinx hits 'Bluey'. To relieve the boredom he's doing some exercises with Bernie Thomas. Bernie slips off Bluey's feet and lands on his nose, causing a temporary blackout, double vision and a little blood to be coughed up. I'm leaning against the wall watching the whole affair as Bernie calls for an ambulance, an ophthalmic surgeon and cold towels. During the game there are three or four female physios in attendance and the two on duty at this stage certainly gained some experience. A couple of hours later, Bluey gets back from hospital, slightly subdued but still with his inevitable wry humour.

In the afternoon, squash with Zap and Rad and a massage by an Austrian masseuse. Excellent job, very relaxing. In the evening, I make a healthy profit at the casino for once. Most of the lads appear at some stage, some to lose, not many to win, and some just to watch the others losing.

TAYLOR   With play washed out, Bernie, Boycs and myself go to the Royal Hobart Tennis Club and play the noble game of real tennis. A very interesting game, but takes a lot of understanding. Naturally Boycs takes it rather seriously – he plays against us with the club pro on his side and every time he wins a point, he's got his hands in the air crowing. He always plays all his sports the same way – win at all costs – and my mind goes back to the time in St Lucia five years ago when the England team had a tennis competition. Chilly played Boycs in the final and while Chilly tried all sorts of fancy shots and drop volleys, Boycs hugged the baseline, playing defensively and watchfully – just like his batting.

Dinner that evening with Jack Simmons, his wife Jacqueline and the commentator Henry Blofeld. Excellent company, wine and meal and Henry gives me a signed copy of his book on the Packer affair. I tell him about an article I'd just read in *The Australian* about the coloured outfits worn by the WSC sides. The West Indians had worn pink in Australia but said they wouldn't wear it when the Packer circus goes to the West Indies in two months, because pink is the 'gay' colour out there! It wasn't till I read this article that I realized why the England side got so many funny looks five years previously when we toured the West Indies under Mike Denness. We were kitted out in pink 'shirt jacks' and we couldn't work out why so many locals were sniggering at us whenever we attended official receptions!

January 21

The rain means the game can't have a proper finish but the final day is illuminated by two amusing incidents. The first involved Phil Edmonds and a bloke called Goodman (known to us all, for obvious reasons as 'Benny'). This fella's a real 'show pony' and when he opens the batting for Tasmania he comes in with his immaculate gear, posing for all he's worth. All of a sudden while the field's getting into place, he hares off down the other end for a practice run! He touches the non-striker's crease and hares off back to the other end. We couldn't believe it and Henri said he'd do the same for a legpull when it was his turn to bat. In he goes, there's nothing on the game, so we're all looking for some amusement. Henri seems to be taking a long time to get his guard sorted out and we're saying, 'He's chickened out.' All of a sudden, with the bowler going back to his mark, Henri sets off on his practice run, to loud cheers from the England squad!

Then the Boycott/Hampshire affair rears its head again. It's the last over of the match, Hampers is batting and there's no

chance of a result. Goose, the acting skipper, sees the funny side of
the situation and brings on Boycs to bowl – which pleases Fiery
because he's always going on about his seven Test wickets and
wanting to turn his arm over. I said to Hampers, 'Interesting
contest, now,' and Hampers said, 'Shall I give him my wicket?' I
said 'Dunno, Hampers, first-class match, don't forget'; he
thought better of it and contented himself with hitting Boycs
for one boundary. At the end, they still didn't speak to each
other . . .

GOWER Boycs had scored ninety not out when Goose declared to
try to get a win, but the game got boring. The crowd wasn't
exactly large but they still dish out the abuse as much as the ones
in Australia, possibly even more, rudely and offensively. They
have a go at JK down at long-leg, he wanted to give it back but the
manager was sitting down there. Later one of our lads had clods of
earth thrown at him . . .

Back to the hotel for a meal, a few drinks and to lose another
fifty dollars at blackjack, despite telling the croupier to deal me
eights rather than tens. Leave for the airport with seventy cents in
my pocket . . .

MURPHY While the team flew to Melbourne for a one-day International, there were several news items to digest. The Australian
selectors had dropped their wicket-keeper Maclean and the
seamer Dymock for next week's fifth Test at Adelaide. The young
Western Australian Kevin Wright takes Maclean's place and the
Queensland all-rounder Phil Carlson comes in for Dymock. Yet
Dymock and Maclean both play in the one-day International
this week!

The England manager Doug Insole refused Kerry Packer's
offer of an invitation match. Insole, presumably feeling it was
merely a WSC publicity stunt, pointed out that the tour itinerary
wouldn't allow it which Mr Packer realized only too well.

One other piece of news with particular interest for the three
Derbyshire players in the tour party: the Northants batsman
David Steele had been officially appointed Derbyshire's new cap-
tain to replace Eddie Barlow.

TAYLOR Some of the lads in the party thought Steele's appoint-ment wasn't a good one because of his defensive batting and general attitude to the game. But I pointed out that he was relatively untried as captain and that he could well be a good choice. I've known Steeley since we first played together for Staffordshire at the age of sixteen, he knows the game inside out and is dedicated to cricket. The club have told him what's expected of him and it'll be up to Hendo, Dusty and myself to ensure he gets the team's support. His batting could be a problem when we play the limited-over stuff, but at the moment what we really need is a middle-order batsman in the Steele mould. His dad lives just across the hill from me at Stockton Brook, so no doubt I'll be seeing a lot of Steeley both on and off the field.

Dymock's unlucky to be dropped for the Test. I think he's a good seamer and he's troubled most of us in the last three Tests. I was impressed with Wright when he kept against us at Perth just before Christmas, even though he bagged 'a pair'. He looks a natural.

GOWER Wright's a very competitive little lad and he's a good choice. MacLean's done well up to a point, but he's rather lived off that 94 he hit against us for Queensland before the first Test. Dusty and Embers have dismissed him six times out of eight with their off-spinners and since the first innings in the Brisbane Test he's never looked like making a run.

We're not bothered about Carlson, we think Dymock's unlucky to be dropped. Carlson's an average performer, with his medium-pace stuff more suited to English conditions. With the bat he didn't enjoy Goose too much in the Queensland match, and we think he'll be vulnerable to the short-pitched stuff.

January 22
Melbourne. A tour record − a rest day with the sun out! At the poolside from 10 am to 6.30 pm accompanied by rather too much beer and wine. Nice to be able to relax completely, but perhaps overdid it this time without trying and end up as history for the rest of the night.

Nets and training next morning and in the afternoon a

reception at Parliament House. The Deputy Premier makes a long speech, then Doug Insole replied with typical wit and brevity, 'Thank you for speaking for not too long, but long enough'. By this time it seemed to me that the only two questions the locals ever asked were what we thought of Australia and their beer. Faced with the first question for the umpteenth time, I'm sorry to say I replied tactlessly but managed to retrieve the situation and smooth things over.

January 24

The one-day International. We stroll it by seven wickets. Terrible wicket, it had just been used for a four-day Sheffield match. There's just no grass on these Melbourne wickets, they're a mudheap. It's blamed on the bad winter and the Rules Football that is played on the ground. Whatever the reason it's not a good cricket wicket, with the ball keeping low or occasionally bouncing. The Aussies bat like a suicide squad. Wood seems to be getting it nearly right despite a couple of pure slogs, when I came up with a touch of the Peter Shiltons, diving to the left and coming up with the ball – doesn't happen all that often!

Border looked in good nick, then dollied a catch to mid-on. Had to sympathize with them in one respect: batting first on a wicket like this, it's not easy to work out what constitutes a good score. In any event they're all out with seven overs left, a cardinal sin in limited-over matches. When we bat, Boycs does an efficient job, Zap looked in good nick before dragging one on and I rode my luck again for the old 'not out'! Hendo gets the man of the match award and the overall performance is typically professional with the bowlers and fielders setting it up for the batsmen. I just hope the next one goes as easily . . .

TAYLOR I didn't fancy sitting around in the dressing room – 'Bluey' was playing in the International instead of me so I lazed around the hotel pool. I'm getting nervous now, not because of the cricket but because I'm due to see Cathy tomorrow in Adelaide. She and the wives of Chilly and Bernie Thomas arrived in Melbourne five days ago and they're now getting acclimatized and waiting for us in Adelaide. I can't wait to see her, even though we've been married for eighteen years. Apart from a weekend in Cleethorpes and Arundel, we've always had the children with us, so this trip is like a second honeymoon.

When I was selected for the trip last September, I told Cathy, 'You can book your passage, you're coming out for the last three weeks.' I'm so pleased for her, because she was always a great comfort in the days when I was permanent reserve to Knotty and she's never complained about me being abroad at Christmas – so this is one holiday she particularly deserves.

Next day when we get off the plane at Adelaide, my hands are freezing cold. Because Cathy's waiting for me at the hotel, I'm like a cat on hot bricks, I'm far more nervous than when I'm playing cricket!

GOWER The plane trip to Adelaide is full of good spirits, the sign of a winning side, I suppose. Chat, my co-diarist, takes some friendly leg-pulling about his wife waiting for him in the hotel. The wives of Dusty and Arkle have to wait another day to fly out from Heathrow, that snow we keep reading about is still a problem and no flights can leave . . .

Six of us – Hendo, Dusty, Both, Chilly, JK and myself – are seated in a row on the plane and with the beers flowing, things get a little boisterous. A bloke in front of us asks Geoffrey Saulez, our scorer, 'What's the average age of your team?' His displeasure is finally compounded by Hendo: 'What's up youth, 'av yer got strop on?' Possibly not the best example of tact but indicative of Hendo's pleasure at being in a winning side, especially after his last disastrous trip to Aussie four years ago. I did sympathize with that chap, though, because a touring side has its own brand of in-crowd humour and it wasn't his fault that he was sat right in the middle of us all.

TAYLOR Cathy and I go with Bernie and Joan Thomas to Mount Lofty Reserve, a koala and kangaroo park outside Adelaide. The first time in four tours I've seen *live* Australian animals – Cathy's influence already proving a beneficial one! Nice to have her with me to break away from the cricket. She's determined to see as much of Aussie as she can and I won't take much persuading to tag along whenever possible. Nice to get away from all-male company – no disrespect to the lads but I'm sure they'd all agree that a woman's company beats a bunch of blokes every time – especially when that woman's your wife!

In the evening it's the Australian Board of Control dinner for the two teams and officials. It started at 7.30 and then it was announced near ten o'clock that the speeches would soon begin. I understand that last year when the Indians came to this dinner, the soup was served at 7.30 and the second course didn't start till twenty to eleven! This time, when the speeches were announced, Hoggy got up and went to the toilet, we assumed. But it was only when Yallop was speaking some time later and praising Hoggy's bowling that I looked around and saw he'd disappeared for the rest of the evening!

GOWER   The Board dinner's one of the better functions. Insole and Brears make lighthearted speeches – Doug as sharp as ever. On my table there's Dusty, Rick Darling, Tom Worrall (a public relations man) and Fred Bennett, who's managed a couple of Australian tours. No struggle for decent conversation . . .

Earlier in the day nine of us turn up at a shopping centre to sign three million autographs, answer questions on the microphone and get a good laugh at the compere. Good PR!

January 26

TAYLOR   The day before the Test, so it's practice in the morning on the best wickets we've yet had on the tour and then I watch Joan Thomas teaching Cathy how to swim in the heated pool.

Some good fun in the afternoon – both teams travel from the ground to the city centre in vintage cars in an early celebration of Australia Day. I was in the leader car with JK, Bernie and the manager, and the owner kept telling us it had taken five days to polish. A sign on the car said, 'Please don't touch, I'm very old and my owner would get upset.' I just had to get a photo taken with the sign across my chest!

In the parade, everyone keeps mistaking me for Brears because of the grey hair and because I'm in the leader car. This has happened throughout the tour. If I'd robbed a bank, I swear Mike would've been done for it! One young lady gives me the come-on look and shouts, 'G'day, Mike' and then a few minutes later, she's further down the road, standing up in her sports car, shouting, 'Nice to see ya, Mike!'

GOWER Good fun in the vintage cars. I did my Hitler impersonation, standing in the back of the car, saluting and shouting, 'We will win! We will win!' I'm not quite sure how that went down, but there was stacks of waving and then we watched some bloke unravel a flag similar to the Australian one!

MURPHY As both sides gathered for their pre-Test dinners, the Australian Board made a significant announcement. Kerry Packer will now be allowed to bid for exclusive rights for his Channel 9 station to cover Tests, the initial point of breakdown with the Board two years earlier. The Board also says Australia will play against any Test team which includes WSC players, although Packer players won't be selected for Australia. It seemed to be a significant, conciliatory gesture by the Board and with the ICC delegates still locked in negotiations with WSC, it looked as if the World Cup was no longer in jeopardy . . .

TAYLOR It's true the Board's announcement marks a positive step forward, but we're getting a little sick and tired of all the talking. People like myself, Goose, Hendo and JK still remain anti-Packer but we're a little disillusioned at the amount of progress being made towards a compromise. Because of this, we aren't going to put the World Cup at risk this summer. It looks as if most people want to see the Packer players in the competition and we realize there's a lot of sponsorship money at stake. And, of course, we know Lord's will want us to go through with it.

GOWER We're pretty certain now that we'll be playing against Packer men in the World Cup. The general feeling among the players is that it wouldn't be right to jeopardize such a competition.

Our team talk tonight is fairly subdued because there's nothing really fresh to say about the opposition, other than go over the points we already know. It's now a question of firing ourselves to perform properly after being away from Tests for a few weeks.

8
Adelaide – Fifth Test

First day

TAYLOR Wicket looks green and Yallop, winning the bleedin' toss yet again, puts us in. We would have done the same – I think Hendo would have had a field day. We cock it up again, only Both looks the part and Hoggy gets the wickets needed to beat Arthur Mailey's record of 36 in a series for Australia against the old enemy.

The best knock of the tour from Both, even if he did run me out. He said he'd called for the fourth run, but I never heard him and I turned round to see him bearing down on me. I had a stab at getting to the other end (groin injury completely healed up, as you've probably just realized!) and I was only four inches out.

We would've been in even worse shape if Hurst hadn't dropped a dolly at long-leg off Mills – that would've made us 27 for 6, but Mills hung on and helped Both salvage something.

In the evening, Hendo bowls superbly and we hit back. Border and Carlson both look petrified as Both digs in a couple of short ones. They play airy-fairy shots and give me simple catches. They should've been grafting away at that stage, waiting for the wicket to lose its moisture.

The real drama comes when Rick Darling is felled by Goose. It was short of a length, kept coming in at him. I thought it had hit him in the box as he rolled to one side, but when we got to him his eyes were open and he didn't seem to be breathing. There were no emotions on his face and Embers turned him over and thumped his chest to get him breathing. Their physio came on, pulled his tongue out and extracted the chewing gum from his mouth to stop him choking on it. He was stretchered off and he's okay, but it scared the life out of me. My legs went weak and my mind went back to the Test in New Zealand when Peter Lever nearly killed Ewan Chatfield with a bouncer. I was in the dressing room when Chatfield was carried in and Lever was crying his eyes out . . .

Bernie tells us we must stop chewing gum while batting in case we're hit and then choke on the gum if we're given artificial respiration. I know it was a fluke injury and nobody was to blame, but incidents like this worry me.

On a lighter note, a lovely meal in the evening with Chilly, Bernie and our wives at a seafood restaurant. Beautiful lobsters and oysters – I told Cathy she mustn't get used to all this rich food!

GOWER Darling's injury was dramatic because nobody knew what he was doing lying there. When a bloke gets hit and lies down, you think, 'Oh, he'll get up in a couple of seconds', next thing I know is that Darling seems to be having a minor fit. Lucky that Middlesex had a pre-season course in medical training last year because Embers knew what he was doing. Bernie Thomas told me afterwards that the ball hit him below the ribs and at the top of the solar plexus and it knocked every last breath out of him.

Back to more pleasant matters . . . the wicket looked too green for comfort at the start, although it's likely to be a good one later on. The Kenny Barrington penknife went in and he reckoned it would last for days.

Hurst bowls excellently – more fire, more pace and confidence than at Sydney and Hoggy bowled two very fast short ones at me when I came in – I didn't see them but I wasn't looking very hard! I felt very confident, the feet were moving well and I was getting behind the line well enough but then Hurst swings one in at me just enough to get me in front of the off-stump.

Boycs edges a good outswinger, Zap gets a nasty lifter that he fends to slip, Arkle chases a wide one and edges to third slip and Brears is unluckily given out, caught off his shoulder. After his dismissal, Brears has lost most of his usual sangfroid. He's certainly not happy and I can easily understand the way I might feel in his position as captain – wanting the side to get a good start having been put in, wanting to get runs himself to silence the remaining knockers and then getting a rough decision.

Both hits some tremendous blows. Unlike my more wristy method, he uses a full swing of the arms to hit the ball very hard. He'll always be able to take people apart with this method but because he can't make late adjustments, due to being committed to the stroke, he will also get out a few times cheaply. But today he gave the ball a hell of a clatter.

Second day

TAYLOR We do well to get them out for 164, considering the wicket's getting better all the time. Both gets another four wickets, what a terrific trier! We trap Darling with the hook shot – he came in, none the worse for last night's ordeal and hit Both for six. Both bowled him a faster one, he went for the hook and it went like a rocket to Goose's safe hands at fine-leg. Higgs and Hurst add 31 for the last wicket, amazing considering they're rabbits with the bat.

When we bat, Brears is out cheaply again – LBW. This time he had no complaints – 'I should've played forward', he says. Arkle gets himself out to the same sort of hook trap we set for Darling. He's struggled for runs lately and is getting a little uptight. We lead by 87 at the close, with eight wickets left and Boycs is looking ominously sound.

GOWER Although Bernie says we shouldn't chew gum when batting, I'm going to carry on – there's no real alternative apart from a spray that only lasts for about ten minutes. Most of the other lads feel the same.

Darling and Wood both pick out fielders in the deep off 'trap' balls. Goose's catch was a good one and Arkle picked up Wood in a specific position for the lap shot off the off-spinner. He was ten yards behind square, a little way in from the boundary in an area where Wood always seems to miscue. A pleasing dismissal.

A good effort to pull back and Yours Truly is very happy with his run-out of Higgs. I just clipped one bail, it tottered slightly and came down in my favour!

Arkle gets himself out again for the second time in the match.

He's got the old problem of deciding what to do with a hook shot that gets him plenty of runs but also gets him out.

So far the batting on either side hasn't been great. Too many have got themselves out, but the struggle's on again and it's a bloody good Test.

In the evening, Goose, JK, Rad and myself and Mr and Mrs Gooch hit Lubo's charcoal grill. Excellent value, inexpensive, and enough red plonk to ensure it's a good spot to eat. Lubo's will always remain in our memories for the huge steaks and plates of kebabs . . .

Third day

TAYLOR Australia Day, National Anthem played as the teams line up before play begins. Must've put us off because we bat terribly. In this heat all we've got to do is stay at the crease and tire out their bowlers but Boycs didn't move his feet (again) and chased a wide one, Gooch somehow gets bowled by Carlson and Lulu tries to pull a long-hop that scurries through and gets him LBW. I join Dusty a quarter of an hour before lunch and my immediate thoughts are of survival. As we come off the field at lunchtime, the Aussies are crowing 'Good session, lads, well bowled Hoggy, well bowled Hursty' loud enough for us to hear. I say to Dusty, 'It's a hot day, we've got to wear them down.'

Throughout the afternoon, we're telling each other, 'Come on, concentrate.' When I'm dropped at slip by Border, Mills gives me a terrible rocket and I do the same to him when he plays a few loose shots just after reaching his fifty, when Hurst beat him a few times outside the off-stump.

Funnily enough, considering the crisis we're in, we score fairly quickly. I tell Dusty, 'Keep the score moving with some quick singles, treat this like a one-day match. Tip and run and we'll tire them out quicker that way.' The score kept ticking along and at no stage were we bogged down. At first national pride was uppermost in our minds, then remembering all the similar partnerships we'd had with our own county, it was a matter of local pride. I reach my first fifty in Test cricket with an all-run four off Bruce Yardley. As soon as I found the gap between mid-on and mid-wicket I shout, 'There's four there – run 'em up!' I was elated for myself and the team.

For some reason, Yallop takes the new ball when the day's at its hottest. Hurst had bowled throughout the pre-lunch session and he was tired. Higgs had bowled his leg-spinners very well and I always prefer the new ball to the spinners, so I wasn't complaining. Hoggy was, though – he complained about a sore thigh and didn't want to bowl. He and Yallop were having words all the time and when we were having a drinks interval they were still at it.

Towards the end, Dusty's given out caught down the leg-side by the keeper. I was in a good position to judge and I reckon the ball bounced before he caught it. An unlucky dismissal but he'd been a great partner.

I walk off the field, absolutely shattered, with 69 not out against my name. I thought, 'We're 280 on now, that'll take some getting.' I had to hang around, waiting to do an interview for the BBC with Chris Martin-Jenkins and when he asked me why suddenly everything had clicked, I told him if I knew I'd make a few more fifties! I just felt confident, used my feet well, had some luck and kept my head down on a good batting wicket. Cathy said it was all due to her timely arrival in Australia but I'm not sure about that one.

A nice casual Perkins reception in the evening. I sit beside Australia's Minister of Sport, can't tell him why I've suddenly found some batting form, and he gives Cathy a book on Australian flowers to end a lovely day . . .

GOWER I saw nothing of Chat and Dusty's great partnership. Goose and Hendo banned me and Both from watching it for superstitious reasons because we weren't watching at the start, just before lunch. So Both and I sat at the back of the dressing room all afternoon, signing millions of autograph sheets and playing 'hangman'. Towards the end, Both popped his head out to have a look at the partnership – and Dusty's out at once!

I'm annoyed at myself for getting out so near lunch. I'd only made two between the two drinks sessions (a gap of forty minutes) but my timing was coming all the time and then Higgs traps me LBW, attempting to pull it to square-leg. Later Boycs tells me I should've been aiming between long-on and mid-wicket, rather than square. He wasn't trying to curb my natural attacking instincts, just suggesting a way of minimizing the risk in playing an attacking shot.

Excellent entertainment at night at the Perkins reception and then at the sumptuous residence of Pat and Maurice Klemich. Ever since Ted Dexter's side in 1962/3, the Klemichs lay on a superb barbecue for the England or West Indian tourists. Tonight it's beef on a spit in a marquee and we're all presented with a nine-inch-high koala teddy! Hendo does a superb impression of a drunk when he goes up to accept his teddy – trousers rolled up, fag never quite finding the mouth and a final trip over the edge of the stage.

Rest day

TAYLOR Very enjoyable lazy time round the hotel pool with Bernie, our wives, Lulu, Boycs and his girlfriend Anne.

A big treat in the evening – vegetables. A Yorkshire friend and cricket fanatic Harry Kershaw entertained us to dinner and he knew how much I'd been missing my veg. In Aussie, you can't, for some reason, get fresh vegetables in restaurants or hotels. The shops sell all sorts but they never find their way onto our tables on this trip. The only one we ever get is chopped-up marrow, like a sort of ratatouille. Harry hears about our dilemma and he and his wife Shirley lay on a superb spread with six types of vegetables, Yorkshire pudding and my favourite sweet of mince-pie and vanilla ice-cream. Can you blame me for not thinking too much about the extra 31 runs needed for my maiden first-class hundred when there are fresh vegetables to eat?

GOWER Didn't fancy an hour-and-a-half drive up to the Borossa Valley for a wine-tasting day – by the sound of it, far too many were going up there. Drank Fiery's wine instead by the pool-side, caught some sun, reeled off some letters and got stuck into a Wilbur Smith novel.

Entertained by the Conways at night and their son, Clive. Very hospitable and flattered by their attitude. Back to bed and phone up Vic at work before kip.

Fourth day

TAYLOR   Embers and I have no problems in the first hour or so and I'm inching towards my first hundred with no alarms. No nervous nineties either, I think, 'I'm now on 97 and I'll hit the ball if it's well up to me and look for some quick singles with some nudges.' Hoggy bowls me a half-volley down the leg-side which I should've smashed through mid-wicket for the necessary four, but I glide it instead, don't play it wide enough and I'm caught behind. I banged my bat on my pad and for a moment I could've cried, but then I realized we were now in a good position to win. Embers comes up, puts his arm round me and says, 'Bad luck, Chat, well played,' and the Aussies congratulate me on the way back to the pavilion. I'm disappointed but not too much, our good position seems to ease the pain that much more.

We leave them 366 to win and Wood again gets run out with Boycs hitting the stumps from mid-on, a great piece of fielding ('I've done it, I've done it!' he kept shouting: he was really chuffed). Wood thought Both had obstructed him because he wouldn't get out of the way. But Both was watching the ball, knowing there was a chance of a run-out and such an incident happens many times in a season. Both didn't make contact with Wood who nevertheless had a hard look at the umpire before going back to the pavilion.

Hughes and Yallop are looking ominously confident at the close. The wicket's playing very well and we'll have to pull something out of the bag to bowl them out.

A disappointing day for me personally, but such feelings are secondary to the pleasure at the prospect of another Test win after such a sticky start. Absolutely knackered at the end of the day, my admiration for the batsmen/keepers like Ames and Knott is now even greater. How they could maintain such standards in Tests behind the stumps and with the bat amazes me. Because of all the running up and down during my six hours at the crease, my knee began to hurt when I kept wicket later in the day. How did Ames, Knott and co. manage to do both for such a long time?

GOWER   Still banned from watching Chat play the rest of his innings but that doesn't bring him any luck. Shame for him, but still a magnificent effort. When I watched some of his innings later on the telly, he made it look so easy, putting us batsmen to shame. He used his feet and played some lovely shots. When I first saw him bat four years ago in a county match against Leicester, he looked the kind of batsman who should regularly get thirties and forties. Perhaps it's a matter of confidence.

Interesting day ahead tomorrow – the way Chat, Dusty and Embers played proved there was nothing wrong with this wicket. We'll have a job getting eight more wickets even if they don't go for the runs.

MURPHY One piece of news that day concentrated everyone's eyes on one man – Boycott. He left it till the last moment of Yorkshire's deadline to announce he would play for the county next season under John Hampshire. It seemed the desire to get some of the credit for building up a good young side was one of the main considerations in his decision. It would have been particularly galling to Boycott if he had left the county, only to see Yorkshire win a trophy with the side he'd moulded. Whatever the considerations, the general feeling was one of relief that the affair seemed to be over and that Boycott might just show the kind of form expected of him in the last fortnight of the tour.

Fifth day
TAYLOR It's a little matter of 95 degrees when we start play, looking for an early breakthrough which doesn't come until after the first drinks session. Hendo bowls Yallop with a beauty – he was bowling over the wicket to the left-hander, the ball pitched off and with Yallop shouldering arms, it held up to hit off-stump.

Lulu takes two great catches – the best one was at backward-point, when he dived to catch a hard slash by Hughes. Goose, after a hard session in the nets, suddenly finds his rhythm and gets Border and Yardley in one over and at the hottest time of the day (two o'clock, 105 degrees) we've won rather more easily than we imagined.

The man of the match award goes to Both for his all-round qualities. I was a little disappointed but consoled myself that I didn't deserve the 'Man of the Series' award in last year's Tests in England against New Zealand. That was a sentimental choice and Both should have won that. So we're evens now, and, more importantly, we'd won again.

GOWER   The crowd for the final day is very disappointing. Have they no faith in their side? When I catch Hughes I let my enthusiasm get the better of me, and end up jumping into Guy's arms. At the time I was very keyed up, thinking to myself, 'This is just the time to rub it in – if anything comes to me in the air, I'm going to dive for it.' I was so delighted when that actually happened but I was embarrassed later when I saw my reactions on TV. It's not my usual style and I didn't want people like 'Annoyed, Neasden' writing to the captain, 'Dear Mr Brearley, would you please restrain your team from kissing and hugging?' I made amends shortly afterwards when I dived to catch Carlson, remembered to curb my enthusiasm and just lobbed the ball back to Chat.

At the presentation ceremony, the microphone packs up for the umpteenth time this tour, and we have to stand around in the baking heat waiting for a replacement mike. Phil Ridings, the Aussies' chairman of selectors, said it had been a very close series, which some of the crowd greeted with howls of derisory laughter!

Fifth Test reflections

TAYLOR   It was a great match for the team and for the Derbyshire trio. Hendo again bowled superbly – all his five match victims were top six batsmen, Dusty again did his all-rounder's duties in fine style and I was pleased with my batting. We received a telegram from our county secretary, David Harrison, and it was nice to think we brought our supporters some good cheer in the frozen Midlands.

I still can't work out why it all suddenly clicked for me with the bat. I just felt confident and I hope this marks a breakthrough for me. Mind you, I batted six hours for 97 three years ago for the International Wanderers in Johannesburg and that innings didn't exactly spur me on to greater things.

It was another great team effort, proving how indefinable is the asset of good captaincy. Poor old Yallop again struggled in the field but he didn't help himself with his bowling changes nor his defensive attitude. The way his side folded up on that last morning wasn't impressive and it smacked of a team with little or no morale. If things hadn't gone our way recently we could be going into the last Test 3–2 down – but we've *made* things go our way.

The Aussie selectors still continue to surprise me – they've dropped Darling for the final Test, yet he's going to play in next week's one-day International. There seems no pattern in their thinking and, at the end of the series, their talented young side still shows no sign of solidity.

GOWER I felt a little sorry for Yallop. He was taking stick from all sides but he seemed to have a better idea of what he was doing than at the start of the series. But in the end it all comes down to the players and how they perform on the pitch and Yallop seemed to have difficulty in getting the best from everyone.

For sentimental reasons, I'd have loved to see Chat get the 'Man of the Match' award, not least of all because Both, being an all-rounder, will surely win some more in his Test career. But it's difficult to assess their respective match-winning qualities in this match.

It was pleasing to see Goose get some of his old fire back on that last day. He's battled away without moaning, fulfilling his duties well as vice-captain and trying to get over his virus. I was happy about my two catches in the second innings, less happy with the stroke I got out to in the second knock but don't see any need for changes in my approach. It was a bad shot, simple as that.

Wright looked a good prospect in his first Test but our assessment of Carlson's fears against the short-pitched deliveries proved correct. In the end they should've done much better in their first innings. The wicket had eased after those first few hours when we didn't bat very well and it was a good chance to build a good lead. But again, their middle-order batsmen let them down.

So it's 4–1 up, one to play and we're in happy humour. One last effort for the Sixth Test is what's needed; 5–1 sounds much better than 4–2 . . .

MURPHY   Once again it was a team effort by England that was the cornerstone of their success. Two recoveries from 27 for 5 and 132 for 6 showed the depth of their experience and their happy knack of finding someone to play above himself in a crisis. In the previous Test it was Randall, this time it was Taylor. The wicket-keeper's batting success delighted many Australians who've come to admire his neat skills with the bat and wondered why he never got the runs he seemed to promise. Boycott said just a few days before the Adelaide Test that Taylor always looked so efficient while batting in the nets that he was surprised he didn't score more heavily – how sound was his judgement.

The Derbyshire partnership between Miller and Taylor wasn't the first time they'd saved England. The previous year, they put on 89 on a turning wicket against Pakistan in Lahore, and they'd supported the fragile Derbyshire batting for several seasons.

Yallop again had an unhappy match. There were no doubts over his place in the side as a batsman (he ended up the only player in the series to score two centuries) but little seemed to go right for him in the field. It seemed mystifying that he should take the new ball half-way through the Taylor/Miller stand when Hurst was out on his feet and Hogg playing hard to get. Then, the following morning, Yallop held back Hogg for 18 overs while Taylor and Emburey consolidated. 'Tiger' O'Reilly, growling in the press box, was advocating the claims of Hilditch of New South Wales as captain, but he hadn't proved his Test quality yet. The one thing that remained in Yallop's favour was the lack of credible alternatives, always assuming the selectors didn't go for experience and give the captaincy to Inverarity.

His opposite number, Brearley, graciously said any of the five Tests could have been won by the other side – and the 62 wickets so far taken by Hogg and Hurst would seem to support that view – but in matters of morale, teamwork and leadership, the gulf simply got wider and wider.

9
Melbourne and Sydney – Final Test

GOWER On the flight from Adelaide spirits are predictably high. Both causes havoc again with his waterpistol, catching the air hostess under the armpit during the safety drill. She heads for the other end of the plane, muttering, 'I'm not coming down here again.' JK, Hendo, Both and myself get stuck into the beers and arrive at the Melbourne Hilton about 6.15 pm. A quick bite and it's next door to the pub till closing time with the above-mentioned plus Goose, Bluey and a couple of Australian pressmen. The cricket highlights come on the TV at 9.30, it's accompanied by cries of exaltation whenever a wicket falls. Might as well grind them into the ground while we can. The good spirits are continued back at the hotel and finally I retire with my room-mate, Hendo. Cups of hot chocolate are summoned from room service, eventually consumed by myself and Bluey because Spike's fallen asleep rather quickly.

Next day end up at the pool on our rest day. It's 41 degrees and just the job. Warmest Melbourne day for a while and pass the time reading Wilbur Smith's *A Sparrow Falls*, good reading with a high content of specialized knowledge built round a decent story line.

February 3
TAYLOR We play Tasmania in a challenge match against the Australian Gillette Cup champions. Before play begins, Hampshire is seen bowling to Boycs in the nets, so one assumes their differences are being patched up.

The game against Tasmania isn't very inspiring, there are only about five thousand in the huge stadium on a dull, damp day. It doesn't compare very favourably with the WSC 'Supertest' final between Australia and the Rest of the World. It's televised from Sydney, and the sunshine's glorious, but I honestly think cricket's reaching saturation point out here, it's always on the television.

At night, Dusty, Arkle, myself and our wives go to the best Chinese restaurant in the city. The Chinese proprietor welcomes us warmly, saying he's a great cricket fan. We have ten courses in three hours and the bill was reasonable. I assume our Chinese cricket fan knocked something off the bill!

GOWER   A complete weather contrast – in one day the temperature's dropped from 102 degrees to 60. The rain comes down. We eventually beat Tasmania by three wickets, but not before some nasty moments – for example, when a ball clears Chilly's head and the keeper and goes for four byes. He called for the old helmet very quickly!

Hendo's doing his escort duty tonight, looking after Both who's worrying about his missus and when she's going to pop their second sproglet. Hendo and Both are good family friends back home, they only live an hour's drive away from each other, so Spike spends some time in his room.

February 4

Another one-day International, this time it's played to a finish and we lose. The wicket was obviously affected by yesterday's rain when we carried on playing at the umpire's insistence – so the wicket was left uncovered for a time. The toss therefore becomes crucial, and when we lose it the struggle is on. Boycs and Zap fend off several nasty lifters from Dymock and at this stage about 160 would seem to be a good score. It's a terrible wicket for such an important game but by the time I come in, about half an hour before lunch, it's playing easier and Cosier and Carlson are on with some 'help yourself' bowling. The wicket begins to play like an English one, i.e. not as much bounce as the Aussie ones, and it suits me down to the ground. Everything seemed to work for me and I start creaming it through the off-side. Both hits hard and provides useful acceleration in the middle of the innings. The ball keeps hitting the middle of the bat and then the fence. At this stage a hundred always seems slightly out of reach and at the start of the last over I'm at the wrong end. Chilly takes a couple of twos and then a one instead of a two, which leaves me with the strike for the last ball and I'm on 97. I made up my mind I was going to hit it through the off-side field if possible and Laughlin bowled it. I give myself that little bit of extra room and flay the ball between deep cover and extra seventy yards away. A great feeling.

I was happier with my Test hundred because it was a bigger struggle and it means so much more, but this one came easier. One coincidence – Chilly was batting with me when I completed my first one-day hundred for England against Pakistan last summer.

They need 213 to win and throughout their innings, I feel our bowlers should be good enough to peg them back. I'm glad when Hughes is out because he's playing well, Toohey hits a good fifty but the real killer is Cosier, who hits 28 in eleven balls, including a huge 6 off JK. Our bowlers let it slip, yet we didn't seem keyed up enough in the field.

The best game of the tour so far, but a shame we lost – it means we've got to play again in a decider.

I'm given the 'Man of the Match' award and asked to say a few words. I've often heard people mumble into the mike so I decide to attack my task like Hitler at a rally. I overdo the volume a little, shout down the mike, thereby distorting the reproduction, so it's almost as bad as whispering. Still, it entertained the lads.

TAYLOR I watch some of the match from the dressing room because Bluey's playing instead of me. I'm disappointed to be left out because I played in England's one-day matches against Pakistan and New Zealand but Brears says he wants to keep me fresh for the final Test. I feel deep down that perhaps I'm being pushed out in favour of Bluey. Nobody's said anything and I may be imagining it, but it'll keep me on my toes.

Lulu's century was magnificent and I thought he'd won us the match. At about 5.15 when Hughes is out, I get permission to take Cathy to mass at the cathedral near the ground, with the game seemingly won by us. When we came out of the cathedral at 7.20, no sooner had I said to Cathy that we'd probably won than a huge roar went up. I knew then that we'd lost because over the years you get to know certain crowd roars and that was certainly an Aussie win we'd just heard.

February 5

GOWER   Hendo and I take it easy in the morning and trundle down to the pool-side late in the morning to embark on a relaxed cocktail-tasting session with Bluey. They disappear very pleasantly, interspersed with dips in the pool and relapses on the sofas.

Later that night an interesting insight into the local licensing laws. I grab two bottles of wine and try to find a restaurant. In that area you have to bring your own wine. They're all closed and I end up back in the Hilton's coffee shop, having to buy a carafe of wine because they're not licensed for 'bring your own' . . .

The next day we play at Geelong, a three-day fixture reduced to one day because of the Internationals. The match ends prematurely just as I'm limbering up to bowl my off-spin in the fortieth and final over. They reach the hundred mark (still sixty short) off the sixth ball of the 39th over and the crowd celebrate the fact by invading the pitch. Brears takes us off the field after checking that we didn't have to go back and bowl again. When the crowd's cleared, their batsmen are still out there, claiming the match. Brears protests and all is resolved when the game's ruled to be of 39 overs' duration, so we're official winners, not that we were really bothered . . .

Randall was good value in the field. He wore a red hat shaped like a tea cosy and when one huge girl ran up to kiss him while he was fielding, he retreated in mock horror at the sight of this gruesome monstrosity. Then to the crowd's great amusement, he let her catch him.

TAYLOR   A bit of a misunderstanding with Brears leaves me upset and wondering if my chances of keeping wicket in the World Cup are receding. Yesterday, Bernie rang up from the team meeting to ask if I was fit to play at Geelong. I was on the toilet and, at my request, Cathy told him the knee I aggravated in the last Test wouldn't allow me to keep wicket at Geelong but that I'd play to give some of the others a rest. I also said I'd be fit to keep in the third and final one-day International.

I asked Bluey to keep wicket today and he said, 'Sure'. At the end of our innings, Brears asks why I'm not keeping wicket and I say, 'Didn't Bernie tell you?' I could tell Brears was upset but it wasn't my fault Bernie hadn't told him what I said. After the game I learn I'm not playing tomorrow in the one-day International and wonder whether I should've bothered playing here today. Perhaps it's my imagination, but for the first time I wonder if Brears thinks I'm telling the truth. I hope he doesn't think I'm playing at picking and choosing because that's not the case — I wanted Goochy to have a match off to be with his wife.

Boycs doesn't help by saying, 'You'll have to watch it — Bluey's a good 'un you know, he'll be after your spot.' I don't know whether Boycs is trying to gee me up or not, but I'll fight for my place. With great respect to Bluey, who's a nice lad, I think I'm a better keeper and I'll try like hell to prove that every time. I dearly want to play for England as long as my standards don't drop.

After the game, we went to a magnificent country club for a dinner reception. Cathy and Joan Thomas have been shown around Geelong during the day and she's got some very good cine film of Timber Tops School where the future King of England had part of his education. I must say the wife's seeing a lot more of Australia than I ever have; when you're a cricketer, it seems one long round of airports, hotels and cricket grounds.

February 7

GOWER We lose the toss in the final one-day International and with it, the game. It's amazing really — tossing the coin is the only part of Brears' captaincy that's let him down on this tour. The wicket's erratic again (it must be the worst looking Test square in the world, with the main part crumbling black soil like a dried river bed). We didn't play well, we lacked application. Brears was the only one to show it — and we're out for 94. Darling and Wood start off like trains, we lose by six wickets and after all the re-scheduling the Aussies have won the Benson and Hedges Cup . . . and don't we know it!

The Aussie side are chirping a lot more than usual, so we pack the bags and leave them to it. We catch the plane to Sydney for the last leg of the tour, with the only real highlight of the match another example of Henri's dry humour. When he was batting he got fed up of Laughlin's persistent wide bowling so Henri removed the leg-stump from the ground and placed it on the edge of the return crease, to the vast amusement of ourselves, the crowd and some of their players – but *not* the square-leg umpire!

On the subject of wide-bowling – when I got my hundred in the previous International six out of eight in Hurst's last over had been short or wide but *none* were called 'wides'. They would have been in England because I had no hope of reaching them. Just shows the differences in interpretations.

Time to kill in Melbourne Airport, so we spend it in the bar. Spirits not down for long, despite having lost the cup and the only danger now is the closeness of going-home time.

February 8
Bluey and I head out to the Royal Sydney Golf Club. A nice-looking course with the clubhouse and rooms immaculately decorated and suitably conservative. Both of us get bored and only endure 14 holes before retiring to the 19th. Golf club showers always seem better than cricket club showers . . .

Later on Hendo, Bluey and I disappear up the Cross and take in some dubious, cheap, amusing and very blue movies before dining out on the pavement with whole chicken, chips and lots of grease. A fair midnight feast. Back in our room Hendo and I can't kick the hot-chocolate habit before sleep. It's a Derbyshire custom that's been introduced to me and it certainly helps you kip.

February 2
TAYLOR   At our team meeting Brears asks us for one last effort so we can win the series handsomely. Boycs is still practising hard for what might be his last Test but there's an overall lethargic air. Boredom's the problem for many – for those of us with our wives here it's easier, but Both, for one, admits he's bored now and just wants to get home and see his family and new arrival. If we can,

we'll bat first and get as many runs as possible and hope the pitch takes spin as it did in the Fourth Test.

We think the Aussies are exaggerating the importance of their one-day victories. Although useful in psychological terms, they're worlds apart from Tests and their selections haven't been consistent enough to give the side that crucial bit of confidence. If we can shake ourselves out of this mood, we'll beat them.

GOWER   The morning practice session wasn't a good one and it's not helped by the Aussies pinching the wicket we were supposed to be using. While we wait to bat on the wicket, we get a good laugh watching Wood practising his running and calling with his new partner, Hilditch. I catch up on my right-hand batting. Goochy throws a few down and it's getting better, I'm developing the off-side shots.

In the afternoon, down to Camp Cove to the topless beach for a couple of hours' voyeurism with JK and Goose. Our team meeting concentrated mostly on attitude – about avoiding any first-day lapses such as at Melbourne and Sydney. We must perform as on the first day at Brisbane. We discuss Hilditch, come to the conclusion he's a plodder, so we must try to stop him anchoring one end while the stroke-makers get the runs at the other end. Not worried about our one-day defeats but if our attitude's not right, we could get stuffed out of sight.

After the team meeting it's downstairs for some snap. The only problem seemed to be a difference of opinion between the manager and our end of the table about how much wine should be consumed. 'I hope the wine isn't being drunk by the people playing tomorrow,' he said. No hassles, really – at my end were Chilly, Rad and Henri, i.e. three reserves.

Hendo and I eventually disappear about 11.30, relaxed but in complete control, only to be told by a group of drunk England supporters, 'Get to bed or you'll never win'. What do they know about it? They don't seem to realize that relaxation's an essential part of the game, otherwise tensions would build up to breaking-point. Some, like Boycs, hardly drink at all, but those who do often are misunderstood. It would be interesting to ask a lot of players what they'd been doing the night before a big innings or great bowling spell. I wonder how many of them were tucked up in bed at 10 o'clock?

Sixth Test, first day

TAYLOR   Yallop wins the toss yet again and bats on a wicket that looks as if it'll turn. They suffer yet another run-out involving Wood, though this time it wasn't his fault. I couldn't understand the mentality of a supposedly intelligent bloke like Hilditch playing the ball to Goochy in the gully and being half-way down the wicket, even though the ball hasn't passed the fielder.

Yallop plays a mixed innings of slogs and good judgement. He also edged a few between gully and third slip but a score of 121 out of 198 speaks for itself. Hughes is out to the last ball before lunch (concentration problems?) and losing the toss doesn't seem a tragedy, especially with Fiery and Brears looking set at the close. A word on the calling by Boz when the coin is tossed – he always calls 'heads'. Don't know why, I bet he wonders after this series!

Some friends from the UK are over here for the cricket – two general sales managers in the hotel pottery business, a leading surgeon at Stoke's City General and two other businessmen, Ernest Mainwaring and Bernard Owen. Cathy and I spend a pleasant evening with them over dinner.

GOWER   The pitch doesn't look bad, fairly easy-paced and Embers gets a few to turn half an hour before lunch, so it should be interesting. The keenness is back in our side, it's Brisbane on the first morning all over again and Botham's gem of a catch at slip to get Wood sums up the performance.

Only Yallop, riding his luck but playing some brave shots, plays at all well. Toohey continues to go through the horrors and Carlson again looks unconvincing against speed, fending a bouncer to slip. At the close Brears and Fiery look secure.

Hendo and I have dinner at night with my cousin Christopher, his wife Diane and friend Pam. Excellent snap in the fish restaurant – oysters, then more oysters, dewfish and *vino blanco*! Very convivial evening, Hendo very amusing – at least to me, but I'm not sure how the rest of the company took to his blunt speaking. We excuse ourselves because of tomorrow's cricket and come back to the inevitable hot chocolate. We manage to order it for the right room this time, unlike last night when it was sent down the corridor and Bluey was woken up. Easy to forget the number of your room after so many hotels.

Second day

TAYLOR We throw away our advantage early on, but then Goochy and Lulu have a fine partnership. Brears gives his wicket away against Higgs and Fiery is given out caught in the slips, although he's not happy about it. Arkle is given out LBW and, sadly, he again shows his displeasure. (Later on he goes and sits on the Hill and gets soaked by some yobs. Who else but Arkle would be so daft as to sit there during a Test, it's just asking for trouble!)

Goochy plays some great attacking shots and just as it looked as if he'll at last get a century and we're talking about a big lead to make us safe, he gets stumped off Higgs. The wicket's beginning to take spin and it's looking rough, but Lulu's playing very well and just when it looked as if he might get a hundred before close of play the rains came down and washed out the last two hours. Within half an hour the ground is completely under water, it was one of the heaviest storms you'll ever see.

GOWER Fiery maintained the ball hadn't carried to slip and although the TV evidence didn't support him, I felt sorry for him. I enjoyed my partnership with Zap – I started well by taking eleven in my first over off Higgs, although my first scoring shot was a sweep to square-leg that wasn't too clever. I've chanced my arm against Higgs a few times this series and generally, felt confident against him.

I was frustrated to see Zap go. He was on for a hundred but lost concentration at the wrong time. When the rains came I felt a little cheated although the new ball was due in five overs' time, which usually means wickets or quick runs. The rain made a magnificent spectacle – it seemed to be funnelled over the ground in one large cloud – and some spectators started playing silly games on the Hill like sliding down on their backsides. About twenty or so played cricket on the outfield in the downpour. Crazy.

Ian and Mary Morris, a retired couple who're friends of my godmother, come up to the bar for a drink and a chat. They're very pleasant, understanding and good company. Hendo and I then disappear into an Italian restaurant down the Cross. Lo and behold, the Radleys and the Goochs are already there. Good large pizzas – mine disappears pronto, Spike's not far behind. Then it's back to the hotel for one more beer and then – suspense – hot chocolate.

Third day

TAYLOR   We get a lead of 110. I bat slowly but confidently for 36 not out (has the Adelaide innings worked the trick?) and Lulu gets a good googly from Higgs that's well caught by the keeper high up on his chest. We use up a fair amount of time, waiting for the pitch to deteriorate and then strike when they bat again. But their first wicket to fall involves me in some controversy . . .

Hendo gets Hilditch to nick one, I dive forward and, in a reflex action, close my eyes. They were shut for a split second and when I open them again, the umpire's got his finger up after the slips had appealed. I didn't appeal and asked the slips, 'Did I catch it?' They replied, 'Of course you did.' What could I do? Yet I'm the one accused of sharp practice.

We got Wood out with some good tight cricket. We tied him down, the crowd got onto him, he lost patience and swished Dusty to Goose at wide mid-off where he took a fine catch. Embers gets the bat/pad routine working to get Toohey and Carlson and they're finished. The crowd were pathetic, they never gave their team any help at all and it was rather sad.

A hectic social evening. Firstly, the Australian Primary Club charity evening, to raise funds for deprived children and then at our hotel, the final reception with Perkins. We've enjoyed these, the food and hospitality have been excellent and it's been very informal.

GOWER   I play rather scratchily and am undone by a good ball from Higgs, which bounced a bit. I can't comment on the Hilditch/Taylor incident – I was down at third man listening to Rod Stewart's band tune up across at the Showground for a concert that night.

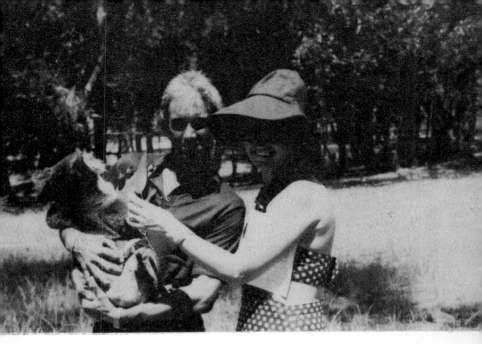

Bob Taylor and his wife Cathy make friends with an inmate of the Nature Reserve near Adelaide on the rest day in the fifth Test (*photo: Bernard Thomas*)

Bob Taylor with the Australian fast-bowling discovery Rodney Hogg after a television interview

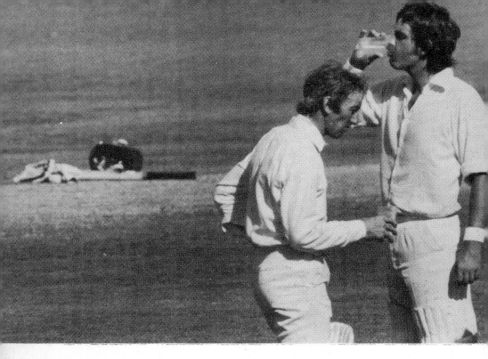

A well-earned breather for Taylor and his Derbyshire colleague Geoff Miller during their vital stand at Adelaide in the fifth Test

Taylor run out on the fourth run at Adelaide in the fifth Test (*photo: Ron McKenzie/News Ltd, Sydney*)

Gower walks in undefeated on 101 in the one-day International at Melbourne; Chris Old is his partner (*photo: Ron McKenzie/News Ltd, Sydney*)

Some Australian-style refreshment for Taylor, Kenny Barrington and Chris Old

The Ashes have been regained at Sydney and it's celebration time for (left to right) Gooch, Hendrick, Taylor, Randall and Old, Tolchard (standing) and Emburey (with stump). Mike Gatting – coaching in Sydney – is in the background (*photo: Patrick Eagar*)

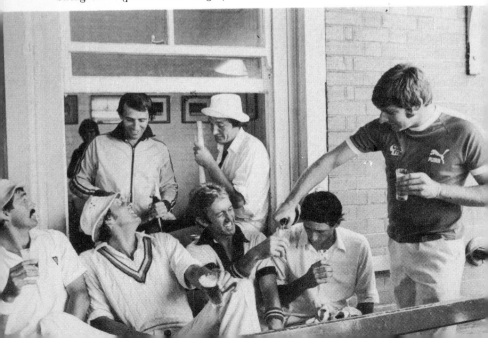

The only batsman on their side who played the correct way was Yardley. Quite rightly he didn't prod around but used his feet to get to the pitch of the ball and then hit it hard. Even when a man was put down at long-off, he still went through with the shot, realizing that if he poked at it he could end up giving a bat/pad catch.

At the end, with the Aussies 70 for 5, the only entertainment comes from a bugler with a good pair of lungs and a nice version of 'The Last Post' and 'When the Saints go marching in'.

After a few drinks at the Perkins reception (where Hendo and I swap name tags to cause confusion) it's off to the house of Sydney journalist Brian Mossop, with Henri and his wife Frances, who's an interpreter at the EEC in Brussels. The main threat in the evening isn't the various kids, more the Mossop's Doberman that prowls around all the time. It's fairly well behaved, although it does bring to mind the final scene in *The Boys from Brazil* where Gregory Peck gets eaten to pieces by half a dozen Dobermans!

Excellent steaks, the best tasted in Aussie. Hendo and I give the beer a crack (it's a rest day tomorrow) and he and I provide cutlery-influenced percussion to the various records. Time passes, the Tooheys beer takes its toll and I retire to the stereo system and collapse to 'War of the Worlds' before Henri gives us the nod and drives us back to the hotel.

TAYLOR   The papers are full of my incident with Hilditch. Bill O'Reilly calls me a cheat and Brears defends me. Unfortunately not many realize I didn't appeal and I wasn't sure whether or not it had carried.

Met Lionel Pickering, editor of the *Derby Trader* and he got his photographer Les Parkin to take photos of Cathy and myself on the rooftop of the hotel which overlooks Sydney Harbour. Lionel tells me that the Mayors of Derby and Chesterfield have organized civic receptions for the three Derbyshire players when we get back, so we're all looking forward to that.

Fourth day
We win by nine wickets. At the start of play we wanted to finish them off quickly because with big hitters like Yardley and Yallop

around they could still set us a difficult target on a turning wicket. Much to our delight, Yallop played inside one that turned as he went down the wicket, he edged it, I caught it and as all wicket-keepers should know, I finished the job by stumping him. Yardley's now the only stumbling block and, to his credit, he played some fine shots. He always looked dodgy against the seamers but here he used his feet very well.

Dusty bowled very well today and we whipped through their batting, leaving just 34 to win.

I've never seen Fiery so nervous as when he went out to open with Brears and to make matters worse the start of our innings is delayed because Yallop wants to bowl with the old ball so he can get more spin. Quite rightly, Boz objected but the umpires over-ruled him. Higgs and Yardley opened bowling spinners and Fiery's caught in the covers. He was terribly downcast when he came back to the dressing room . . .

Arkle typically ended the series on a bizarre note. He got all the team to autograph his bat with a black felt-tip pen on its face and he had to go out and play a couple of balls with the autographs facing the bowler! He gets the last laugh though, because a cricket collector gives him 75 dollars for it.

So we've won again and with the champers all over the place, players swop caps, sweaters, ties and blazers. I didn't bother because I've got all mine from previous tours.

A lovely end to the series in the evening when Cathy and I, Bernie and Joan and Goochy and his wife went along with Goose and his girlfriend to see Joan Sutherland at the Opera House in *The Merry Widow*. Talk about going out from the series on a high note.

GOWER Before the start Brears reminded us we might still have to bat and that the game still had to be won. But there was an end-of-term feeling and only Brears and Boycs had a net.

The biggest excitement came before we began to bat, when Yallop said he wanted to start with the old ball. Brears told the umpire he wanted Yallop to take the new ball. The umpire said that there was nothing in the rules to stop Yallop, and Brears said that was ridiculous. Doug Insole agreed with Brears, but it was only after the game started with Yardley and Higgs turning the old ball square that we found the relevant rule that either captain may claim the new ball. We thought about informing the umpires and starting our innings all over again but nothing was done. It was also suggested that someone should ring up Donald Carr, the TCCB secretary at home, to get a ruling – after all, it was only about three in the morning UK time!

The situation wasn't without its humour, though – Henri said to Boycs, 'Now here's your chance to get at the spinners, you've been moaning all tour that you've never seen them!'

Fiery's not a happy man in the dressing room when he's out. He desperately wanted to finish on a high note and he's completely dejected. Yallop for once doesn't make rash statements, although it wouldn't have surprised us to hear him still say, 'We can do it, we can do it.' One has to give him some sympathy, though – the press and public are down on him, yet he's the only player on either side to score two centuries this series.

En route from the presentation, some bird slips me a small present – a bottle of Vaseline Intensive Care lotion which 'protects your suntan', says the blurb. Her note refers to an interview I did during the Adelaide Test when my sun-tanned legs were getting full exposure.

Beer's flowing in the dressing rooms, all tension has gone and the Aussies don't show any obvious despondency. After defeat they become almost normal but when they're on top, there's no holding them.

The Western Australia lads have a plane to catch back to Perth so we bid them farewell and with Hendo at the wheel (exceptionally sharp with the brakes) we go back to the pub. Continuing the revelry entails strolling down to the other end of the Cross to an establishment called 'The Bourbon of Beef' or something similar. We get there at six, twelve cans of Foster's appear on the bar, the juke box belts out music and the session is on. The atmosphere is alcoholic and mostly silly, the only attempts at seriousness come later on when alcohol prevents one realizing just how much rubbish one's talking or sagely listening to.

Hendo is the first to flake out at 7.30, Bluey and JK follow later and we're joined by Hoggy, who's as dry-witted as ever and not averse to drinking our beer. Guy's well gone; Brears, Insole, possibly some others arrive but seem to fade. Eventually I decide to try to make it back to the other end of the Cross. Only a couple of minor words with some of the ladies of the night and I get back to seek out Fiery to look at some proofs done by Ron McKenzie, a photographer.

Next day I wake at 6.30, feel ten times more clear-headed than the previous night and sit in the bathroom for an hour and a half, avoiding waking Hendo, and looking at the proofs with markedly more appreciation that the night before. Nip into town with Hendo in Brears' stationwagon to get some prezzies for his kids. We get some rocket burners and test them back at the hotel. Will they still be in one piece by the time Hendo gets home?

At 5 o'clock, presentation of clocks to Kenny Barrington, Bernie and the manager. Also discussion re Packer and the Cricketers' Association meeting in April. Most seem very much against him and proposals are worked out that no new Packer players should be approached by county clubs.

February 17
Goochy and his missus disappear to Perth, where he's due to play club cricket there with his county colleague, Ken McEwan. Not quite what I'm looking forward to . . .

TAYLOR   Everyone catching up with their souvenir shopping and sunbathing. Twelve of us go out to the home of a British Airways pilot friend, Rod Berkley. It's about twenty miles out of Sydney and I got the route mapped out. Goose, a little worse for his celebrations, said he knew the way, so I gave him the directions list to make sure and told him I'd follow in a carload. Goose's navigator was a high-spirited Botham and as soon as we passed over the Harbour Bridge they shot off without us. So we're now completely in the dark but with Chilly in excellent form as the navigator, we pieced together the roads and suburbs I jotted down and we got there fifteen minutes before Goose and Both!

February 18

GOWER   Panic packing. Bags ready by 10.30, then there is time to kill. Not enough sun to make the beach worthwhile, so watch the midday movie on the box. Arkle's worried about getting up to Nottinghamshire in the snow and he goes and rings up his transport – the equivalent of two in the morning in the UK! He's ecstatic at the prospect of going home and seeing his wife and kid again and he keeps telling me, 'Just you wait till you have one of your own!'

On the bus I sit at the front and try doing the posh BBC compere bit as each passenger walks in. I describe what the ladies are wearing and the attributes of the lads. We hit the airport bar, the plane's delayed – what a shame! A couple of phone numbers are exchanged, some for social reasons, some also in case of emergency for benefit do's!

Our party is split up all over the plane and I end up sitting next to a couple who've been running an orphanage in Newcastle for the last eight years – seemed true to type! I catch some kip during the film (plane movies invariably have that effect on me!) and emerge for a final noggin before getting off at Singapore Airport with Chat and Cathy, Bernie and his wife. I leave the rest of the party *en route* for the duty free.

I'm met at Singapore Airport by Corinne Kilbee, the wife of my host for the next fortnight, and the others make their way to their hotel. Coming up – a fortnight of complete relaxation . . .

10
Reflections on the tour

GOWER I enjoyed the tour both socially and professionally. Early on I was a little worried about my batting but the century in the Perth Test came at just the right time. Considering the state of most of the wickets, I was happy with my overall performance. I know I was out playing shots a few times, but you don't get runs unless you play shots and I see no need to alter that belief. Because of the extra bounce on the Aussie wickets, I tended to dwell a little on the back foot to avoid getting tucked up and 'gloving' it to the keeper, and that seemed to work most of the time.

The wickets were a big disappointment. From what I'd seen the previous year in Western Australia and heard from experienced players, they were a great surprise. There were very few decent wickets that gave the bowlers and batters an equal chance. Melbourne was the worst – we never played well there at any stage of the tour. The bounce disappeared in no time and the ball kept low too often. The ball turned too quickly at Sydney and although Adelaide rolled out easy-paced, I can't think of many days throughout the series when the wickets were good and flat.

Obviously the wickets didn't help the scoring rates and predictably we got a lot of stick for taking our time to get the runs on certain occasions. At Sydney in the Fourth Test and at Adelaide the press said we should be smashing the ball out of sight, but they missed the point: time was then more important than runs and we needed to occupy the crease to let the wicket deteriorate when they batted *and* avoid giving them too much time to get the appropriate runs. The Aussie press badly wanted a successful national side but we weren't going to throw away Tests just to please them.

Two months after the end of the tour, I'm still convinced 5–1 was a false result. The talent was in the Aussie side but their defects dogged them at crucial times; at no stage did their first five batsmen come good in the same innings, there was a general lack of application when things weren't going well, they never had a Test class all-rounder and commonsense let them down on occasions – witness the running between the wickets of their openers, which was legendary by the end of the series.

Yallop inevitably got some stick for the defects of the team. But someone had to be thrown in at the deep end after Simpson retired and he did get better towards the end of the series. Inverarity may be a shrewder skipper but you have to equate his ability as a Test player with Yallop's and there's no doubt that Yallop was worth his place as a player. He looked suspect early on against pace (don't we all?) but he played the spinners better than anyone on his side. Toohey was disappointing but he looked a good player the previous summer and you don't lose it just like that. Like Doug Walters, you have to accept his weaknesses if you want his strengths – despite his scoring potential, he was vulnerable outside the off-stump against the pace bowlers and didn't play our off-spinners very well either.

Hogg and Hurst impressed me; Hogg bowled well throughout the series and his large total of LBWs shows how remarkably accurate he was. He proved a lot of people wrong, especially those who said his good performance in the State game was a fluke. His asthma didn't seem too much of a worry – though he did seem to have some problems with his captain. Hurst got better and better as the series progressed. From the Fourth Test onwards he bowled a yard quicker and his confidence was boosted by his 5 for 28 in our first innings at Sydney.

Inevitably the Packer affair overshadowed events, although we didn't feel it affected our cricket. We wanted larger crowds, of course, and we were conscious of the success of World Series Cricket, but we felt our priority was a convincing win in the series. It wasn't our fault that the crowds stayed away towards the end – are we to blame because the Aussies don't like a losing side?

Packer was only discussed once in a meeting of all the players.

That came at the end of the tour in Sydney when Brears called us together to discuss our feelings. Goose had instigated the meeting because back home the Cricketers' Association wanted to know our feelings about boycotting the World Cup if Packer players were involved. The general feeling was that it seemed stupid to spoil the World Cup. People like Hendo, Chat, JK and Goose are more anti-Packer than others in the party, although Brears was pressed for his views – summarized they are, 'We've built up a good side here and it would be a shame to spoil it, i.e. don't sign for Packer.'

At no stage on the tour was I officially approached by WSC and it would have taken a fairly extraordinary offer to make me consider signing. I don't have a great regard for the kind of cricket involved – although I don't discount the element of competition in their matches. Whenever I've watched it on the TV, it's never really looked right and after my experiences on this tour, I wouldn't fancy the prospect of being relegated to the country circuit to play games for Packer. I'd miss Test cricket greatly plus the kind of team spirit we enjoyed on this trip and commercially things look bright for me under the umbrella of established cricket.

Many people said that we wouldn't have beaten the Aussies so handsomely if we'd had to play their side containing Packer players. That may be so and they do have some fine cricketers on their books, but one can never be sure and I'll settle for beating the side that's selected to play us. How can we possibly assess such imponderables?

We were a happy team off the field. All credit to the management – Doug Insole was very impressive. He didn't seem to crack up at any stage, he dealt with the politics calmly, he's a funny bloke, a good PR man, a dry wit, dangerous behind the wheel of a car and an implacable murderer of oranges!

His assistant, Kenny Barrington, was good value as well – not least in his unconsciously funny moments. I shan't forget his 'Smorgas Gas Board' remark in a hurry, nor his revelation to Hendo in the nets that he'd got the batsmen in 'two man's land'! His conviction that everything was 'a bleedin' knockout' remained constant and he was always there with encouragement and advice. In the dressing room he was like a player, worrying his guts out and it was great to see him wheeling away his leg-spinners in the nets. A great enthusiast and character.

Bernie Thomas was officially the physiotherapist but he seemed to do everything. A real 'Mr Fixit' – he knows a lot about most things: commerce, fitness, cameras, exchange rates, where to get bargains. He admits cricket's not his speciality but his advice on attitude to the game was invariably sound.

The skipper, Mike Brearley, combined authority with sociability. There was no sign of aloofness, even though I didn't see a lot of him in the evening. He was a sane person to be in charge – didn't flap under pressure and knew when to hand out rollickings – i.e. at Sydney in the Fourth Test. It was interesting to compare him with Illingworth, my skipper at Leicester. Both are very good tacticians, but Illy has a sterner attitude. Their contrasts probably reflect where they've played their cricket, rather than any tactical reasons. I was impressed with Brears' imaginative field placings, especially to the spinners. He often had a 7–2 field for Dusty and Embers, with just a mid-off and cover, and he seemed to have that indefinable knack of anticipating a mishit and putting a man in that position.

Bob Willis, the vice-captain, did well to keep his depression about his own form and fitness away from his duties. An interesting contrast to Brears as skipper – he'd wield the big stick on the field if necessary, although he maintained a sense of humour. A very confident character, straightforward, with a good cricket instinct. He gave me some sound advice if I ever skipper a side: 'If you think of something, just do it, don't hang around wondering if the time is right.'

My final thought on the tour – the best moment. There were two of them and they both involve my centuries. The first at Perth when Hurst bowled the ideal length on my leg-stump and then at Melbourne when I hammered Laughlin through the off-side. Both shots were off the middle of the bat and I enjoyed seeing the ball clatter to the pickets. A great, indefinable feeling – and I hope I'll have a few more before I finish . . .

TAYLOR   It was the happiest tour party I've been with. Our management were first-rate (they didn't accept every social invite, for example, this helping to cut down on the earbashing) and everyone seemed to blend well on and off the field.

I was happy with my own form behind the stumps, apart from a few minor blemishes, and delighted with my batting. I've got a challenge on to hang on to my number-one spot and it's up to me to maintain my standards.

I was disappointed with the Australians. They weren't captained very well and their overall air in the field wasn't a patch on earlier Aussie sides I've played against. Their best players lost concentration at vital moments – Kim Hughes was the worst offender – and the selectors didn't do them any favours either by chopping and changing the side.

The wickets were indifferent compared to previous tours and the net facilities were consistently poor – nets are very important to someone out of form. I'm sure the groundsmen had problems with the weather, and in the case of Sydney, just too much cricket was played on the ground. But there were some good points from the tour – the use of helmets for a start. I'll never be without one whenever I bat and I hope my improved form will continue now I've got that inner confidence you have when you know you're well protected about the head.

I saw nothing to change my views about World Series Cricket. As far as I'm concerned there's nothing to touch Test cricket and that goes for most of our team. Packer can teach us a lot in television techniques and there's no doubt his threat has led to better financial rewards for players staying with established cricket, but I'd never be tempted by him. I still feel there should've been some announcement on the progress or lack of it towards a compromise during our tour. All we heard were a few nods and whispers. Surely there's been enough talking done to hammer out a solution? That's one of the reasons why I agreed we should let the World Cup go ahead as planned. Why should the sponsors and players lose out, when we're still in the dark?

Financially we did very well out of the tour. The perks pool worked well and the players cleared £1,500 each from prize money, personal appearances and adverts – this in addition to our basic tour fee. Before we left England I said the perks pool mustn't interfere with our play in the way that it seemed to with the Scotland World Cup team last year – and at no stage were the various commercial activities intrusive.

I thought Doug Insole and Kenny Barrington were terrific in their differing ways (and I shan't forget Insole's Inspector Clouseau on Christmas Day) and Bernie Thomas was great as well. He was a terrific comfort to me when my groin injury flared up and he seemed to get so many things organized – hotel accommodation, flights for our wives and endless other things. And the fact that there were hardly any muscle strains among the squad proves how good were Bernie's training routines.

Mike Brearley was the best skipper I've known. Quiet and firm, and although intellectually remote from me, never 'talked down'. He had all the necessary qualities as captain, apart from being an automatic choice as a player on merit – and I think he should stay in the side as captain as long as we're successful because that's partly due to his abilities as a leader. Like most of us he's commercially minded, yet he'll do all the charity work that's going. A nice man.

The responsibility of being vice-captain calmed down Bob Willis a lot compared with other tours, when he was a bit of a lad. The influence of his girlfriend, Julie, helped as well, I'm sure. He was very good in PR terms on this trip, he spoke well and was always affable, despite his own personal worries. He was amusing, dry, and enjoyed a good relationship with Brears. He seemed to read the wickets better than anybody else – and no need for the Kenny Barrington penknife.

My outstanding memory's an easy one and it's got nothing to do with the cricket. It was when my wife Cathy opened the hotel-room door in Adelaide. I didn't want to be embarrassed in front of the players and I told her to stay in the room till I arrived from Melbourne. Having her there with me for the last three weeks set the seal on a marvellous tour.

MURPHY   The team were a success on and off the field. By common consent, they were one of the most approachable and good-natured parties to tour Australia in recent years.

Gower delighted the neutrals (and, one suspects, the committed Australians) with the quality of his strokeplay and to score more runs and have a higher average than anyone else on either side was a fine effort. But Gower's charm as a batsman doesn't reside in statistics and his two centuries were the highlights of a tour where the batting was rarely distinguished.

Taylor was his usual immaculate self. In the words of Ken Barrington, 'He's so good you almost forget he's there.' He proved an ever-popular tourist, a great advert for the game and a much-improved batsman. His footwork against the spinners during his 97 at Adelaide was as good as anything offered by the accredited English batsmen.

The crowds were disappointing – due in part to the failings of the Australian side, the heat, the sheer saturation of cricket by the media and, of course, the rival World Series Cricket. Test attendances were half that in 1974/5 and the Packer matches were much more successful through the turnstiles than the previous summer.

Slow scoring was also blamed for the disenchantment with the Ashes Tests. England especially was singled out for blame in this respect, which was true up to a point but ignored the fact that they often needed to claw their way back into a game before building a platform to attempt victory. On the third day of the final Test, England scored 92 runs in 223 minutes – but they had already decided to occupy the crease as much as possible to enable the wicket to wear, so it would take spin. The plan worked perfectly. In the end Australian criticism of the English scoring rate surely stemmed in part from irritation at their successful methods.

The feeling persisted – and it was confirmed by the England players – that there was little to choose between the two sides. If the Sixth Test had begun with either team ahead by 3–2 it would not have been surprising. Each had three 'Man of the Match' winners in the series, and the Australians scored four centuries to England's two. Hogg and Hurst took 66 wickets to the 62 of Willis,

Botham and Hendrick; and Darling, for example, only scored 32 runs less than Boycott who played in two Tests more. But English reslience, morale and sheer canniness seemed to tell in the last third of the match; often the Test was poised evenly over the first few days, only for Brearley to tighten the crews and pull England clear.

Australia didn't help themselves with unforced errors. Six times a run-out broke their opening partnership, ten times an Australian was run out, compared with England's two. Granted that some of the run-outs were the product of good fielding, but the disparity is still instructive.

Furthermore the talented Australian batsmen had the habit of throwing their wickets away when apparently well set. No player exemplified this more than Hughes: time after time he'd suffer a rush of blood to the head immediately after an interval, a drinks session or even when a new bowler came on. A classic example was in the Fourth Test – England 152, Australia 126 for 1 with Hughes and Darling going smoothly and two England bowlers about to be laid low with illness and heat exhaustion. Instead of building an innings, Hughes throws his wicket away to the first ball after lunch to the astonished Willis.

The difference between the captains was, of course, vital. Even though he won the toss eight times out of nine when opposing Brearley, Yallop wasn't in the same class. His field placings were invariably negative, he seemed lax with some of his players and appeared to miss out on those little tactical ploys that distinguish a good captain. Nobody in the England dressing room could understand why Yallop didn't bring on the leg-spinner Higgs whenever Botham came in. He always struggled against the ball leaving the bat, Higgs dismissed him four times in the series – yet the penny never seemed to drop with the Australian captain.

There were other important differences between the two sides – a long Australian tail, their lack of a class all-rounder, an inability to play the English off-spinners, inferior fielding and England's knack of finding someone to get them out of a self-imposed crisis. The Australian selectors have had more inspirational summers as well. Border's reward for a splendid couple of innings on Sydney's turning wicket in the Fourth Test was to be dropped for the final one. Maclean should've made way for the younger, more agile Wright before the Fifth Test, once his batting weakness against off-spin was discovered. Darling, Cosier, Laughlin and Dymock were in the successful side in the last one-day International . . . yet they didn't play in the final Test three days later! Perhaps if Yardley had been selected to bowl his off-spinners on the turning Sydney wicket in the fourth Test, perhaps if Dymock had been on hand to bowl his seamers at Brisbane . . . perhaps, perhaps. It's so easy to be wise after the event and one can sympathize with the selectors as they saw so much talent creamed off by World Series Cricket. But there's no doubt England selected more wisely.

In the series, there was too much gamesmanship, the umpires were put under too much pressure (and occasionally buckled), and the overall quality of the play wasn't high. But for the England players it was a memorable one. And for Brearley – with eight Test victories against the ancient enemy in just two series – it was a triumph that will take a fair bit of equalling.

APPENDIX

Statistical summary of the tour

by ROBERT BROOKE
Association of Cricket Statisticians

Statistical summary
of the tour

Bob Taylor set a new record for dismissals by an England wicket-keeper touring Australia. His 42 victims put him two ahead of Alan Knott from the 1974/5 tour – Knott took three more on the New Zealand part of the tour to give him the all-time record of 43. But Taylor didn't have the games in New Zealand on this occasion to add to his tally.

Taylor's Test record as a wicket-keeper is 59 dismissals in 19 Tests up to the end of the tour to Australia. He is the only England wicket-keeper with a Test career of an average of more than three dismissals per Test, and his average of 3.11 is beaten only by four Australians:

R. W. Marsh   – 198 dismissals (average 3.81)
G. R. A. Langley – 98 dismissals (average 3.77)
H. B. Taber   – 60 dismissals (average 3.75)
A. T. W. Grout – 187 dismissals (average 3.67)

and West Indian F. C. M. Alexander – 90 dismissals (average 3.60).

The nearest Englishmen are:

A. P. E. Knott – 252 dismissals (average 2.83)
A. F. A. Lilley – 92 dismissals (average 2.63)
J. T. Murray   – 55 dismissals (average 2.62)

A. C. Smith exceeded Taylor's present average but played in too few Tests for this to be fairly compared.

Taylor's 97 in the Melbourne Test means he's within sight of being only the second player to score 10,000 runs yet never a hundred. His tally at the end of the tour in first-class matches was 9,536. Only Tony Lock has ever 'accomplished' this feat.

There is a strong case for David Gower to be regarded as having made the most promising start ever by an English batsman in Australia. His Test figures are better than any English batsman in Australia of a similar age. The only one in any way comparable is M. C. Cowdrey, who in the 1954/5 Test series had the following figures:

5 matches: 9 innings; 0 n.o.; 319 runs; 102 h.s.; 35.44 average

Cowdrey, in fact, reached the age of 22 during the tour, whereas Gower was 22 on 1 April. To find a younger England batsman with comparable figures on his first Australian Test tour one has to go back to J. W. Hearne. In 1911/12 he celebrated his 21st birthday during the Fourth Test and his record for the series was:

5 matches: 9 innings; 1 n.o.; 281 runs; 114 h.s.; 35.12 average

By way of comparison with other English batsmen in their first series in Australia, one can quote the following post-war records, players under the age of 28 only included:

		M	I	N.O.	Runs	H.S.	Average
T. W. Graveney	1954/5 Age 27	2	3	0	132	111	44.00
G. Boycott	1965/6 Age 25	5	9	2	300	84	42.86
A. W. Greig	1974/5 Age 28	6	11	0	446	110	40.55
P. B. H. May	1954/5 Age 24	5	9	0	351	104	39.00

The best record of all time for an English batsman in his first series in Australia was achieved by W. R. Hammond in 1928/9 at the age of 25:

M	I	N.O.	Runs	H.S.	Average
5	9	1	905	251	113.12

For all Test cricket, Gower's record before his 22nd birthday is considerably better than that of any of his English predecessors. Gower's Test figures, at the end of the Australian series, are:

M	I	N.O.	Runs	H.S.	Average
12	19	1	858	111	47.67
					(2 hundreds)

The only England players who scored 400 runs before their 22nd birthdays are:

J. N. Crawford   469 runs (average 22.23)
D. C. S. Compton   468 runs (average 52.00 – 2 hundreds)
J. W. Hearne   431 runs (average 30.79 – 1 century)

Gower's first-class county average of under 30 has been remarked upon in some quarters, but it is by no means unique for a batsman to tour Australia with so comparatively low an average. M. C. Cowdrey was averaging well under 30 for Kent when he first toured Australia in 1954/5.

Ian Botham's achievement in scoring more than 250 runs and taking more than 20 wickets in the series is the first time this has been done in an England/Australia series since 1920/1, when J. M. Gregory scored 442 runs and took 23 wickets for Australia. The only time an Englishman has achieved this record was in 1901/2 when L. C. Braund scored 256 runs (36.77) and took 21 wickets (35.14). G. Giffen, in 1894/5, with 475 runs and 34 wickets for Australia, is the only other player to have performed this feat in a series.

R. M. Hogg's 41 wickets in the series is the highest ever for Australia in a series against England, beating A. A. Mailey's 36 in 1920/1 and is second only to J. C. Laker's 46 in 1956 as the highest for either side in a series. It is, however, the highest total for any Test series in Australia and second to Grimmett (44 v. South Africa in South Africa 1935/6) as the highest for Australia anywhere. Of Hogg's 41 wickets, a total of 23 were from the top six in the batting order.

Graham Yallop's 121 in the final Test represents 61.1 per cent of his side's total. Only four other batsmen have beaten this percentage in a completed Test innings – Bannermann, Greenidge, Reid and Nurse.

In the series, Australia managed 24 'ducks', an all-time record (18 was the previous highest). Alan Hurst set an unenviable record with the bat – he became the first Test player to get six noughts in a series!

FIRST MATCH v. SOUTH AUSTRALIAN COUNTRY XI AT RENMARK

England		
J.M. Brearley	c Madden b Magarey	29
G.A. Gooch	st Madden b Magarey	47
C.T. Radley	c Ellis b Robinson	64
D.I. Gower	b Treloar	26
D.W. Randall	not out	23
R.W. Tolchard	not out	5
G. Miller		
C.M. Old		
M. Hendrick		
J.K. Lever		
J.E. Emburey		
	lb 2 nb w 1	5
	Total (4 wkts decl)	199

S. Australian Country XI		
G. Madden	c Emburey b Miller	11
L.K. Bowey	b Old	31
I.J. Fillery	b Emburey	35
R.J. Ellis	c Tolchard b Hendrick	10
B.J. Sampson	c Radley b Randall	37
W.L. Darling	run out	6
G.A. Wyman	not out	2
P. Magarey		
D. Treloar		
A. Robinson		
D. Cutting		
	lb 4 nb 1	5
	Total (6 wkts)	137

Bowling

S.A. Country				
Treloar	8	0	45	1
Wyman	8	0	43	0
Cutting	6	0	34	0
Magarey	10	0	59	2
Robinson	4	0	13	1

England				
Hendrick	8	3	31	1
Lever	3	0	12	0
Miller	6	3	16	1
Old	6	2	6	1
Emburey	7	0	33	1
Gooch	3	0	27	0
Randall	1	0	7	1

Match drawn

SECOND MATCH v. SOUTH AUSTRALIA AT ADELAIDE

South Australia	*(First Innings)*		*(Second Innings)*	
J.E. Nash	lbw b Miller	124	st Taylor b Miller	33
W.M. Darling	c Miller b Willis	17	c Edmonds b Old	1
I.R. McLean	c Taylor b Edmonds	30	c Sub (Randall) b Miller	52
B.L. Causby	c Brearley b Miller	20	c & b Edmonds	4
J.L. Langley	st Taylor b Edmonds	1	st Taylor b Edmonds	0
R.K. Blewett	c Taylor b Willis	22	b Edmonds	12
P.R. Sleep	c Taylor b Lever	45	c Taylor b Edmonds	3
T.J. Robertson	c Taylor b Willis	2	b Edmonds	24
R.M. Hogg	b Lever	11	run out	16
G.R. Attenborough	lbw b Miller	19	run out	3
A.T. Sincock	not out	14	not out	1
	b 2 lb 2 nb 2	6		
	Total	311	Total	149

Bowling

Willis	11	1	61	3					
Lever	16	1	67	2	Old	5	1	20	1
Old	18	2	78	0	Lever	9	0	40	0
Edmonds	21	5	53	2	Edmonds	21	3	52	5
Miller	18.4	5	41	3	Miller	16	2	37	2
Gooch	1	0	5	0					

England XI	(First Innings)		(Second Innings)	
G. Boycott	lbw b Hogg	62	lbw b Hogg	6
G.A. Gooch	c Robertson b Hogg	4	b Sleep	23
C.T. Radley	hit wkt b Hogg	4	c Sleep b Sincock	3
D.I. Gower	lbw b Attenborough	73	c Blewett b Sincock	50
J.M. Brearley	b Sincock	27	run out	25
G. Miller	c Langley b Hogg	0	lbw b Sincock	5
R.W. Taylor	c Blewett b Sleep	6	c Langley b Attenborough	4
P.H. Edmonds	not out	38	c Robertson b Attenborough	0
J.K. Lever	c & b Sleep	1	b Hogg	28
C.M. Old	c Darling b Sleep	4	c McLean b Sleep	40
R.G.D. Willis	absent injured		not out	0
	lb 5 nb 8	13	b 4 lb 1 nb 7	12
	Total	232	Total	196

Bowling									
Hogg	12	2	43	4	Hogg	12.4	1	39	2
Sincock	9	0	42	1	Sincock	10	2	28	3
Attenborough	15	1	49	1	Attenborough	11	2	49	2
Sleep	17.5	3	72	3	Blewett	5	1	19	0
Blewett	10	4	13	0	Sleep	12.5	1	49	2

South Australia won by 32 runs

THIRD MATCH v. VICTORIAN COUNTRY XI AT LEONGATHA

England XI			Victorian Country XI		
G.A. Gooch	c Roberts b Salmon	29	K. Roberts	b Hendrick	3
G. Miller	c & b Carroll	30	S. McNamara	c Gooch b Emburey	20
D.W. Randall	c Challis b Carroll	7	I. Eddy	c Radley b Hendrick	0
C.T. Radley	c McNamara b Aitken	1	A. Sperling	b Edmonds	6
D.I. Gower	c Salmon b Aitken	21	R. Joseph	st Taylor b Emburey	0
R.W. Tolchard	b Aitken	0	T. Carroll	b Emburey	4
R.W. Taylor	c McNamara b Aitken	21	B. Wrigglesworth	run out	8
P.H. Edmonds	not out	10	G. Challis	st Taylor b Miller	6
J.E. Emburey	c McNamara		N. West	c Gooch b Emburey	0
	b Wrigglesworth	3	C. Salmon	c Radley b Emburey	0
M. Hendrick	not out	2	C. Aitken	not out	5
R.G.D. Willis					
	b 5 lb 1	6		b 5 lb 2	7
	Total (7 wkts decl)	130		Total	59

Bowling									
Victorian Country					England				
Challis	7	0	22	0	Willis	3	1	9	0
Salmon	7	0	32	1	Hendrick	6	2	10	2
Aitken	15	4	30	4	Emburey	11	6	10	5
Carroll	8	0	24	2	Edmonds	7	0	16	1
Wrigglesworth	6	1	16	1	Miller	2.4	1	7	1

England won by 71 runs

FOURTH MATCH v. VICTORIA AT MELBOURNE

Victoria	*(First Innings)*		*(Second Innings)*	
J.M. Wiener	c Edmonds b Lever	48	not out	14
P.A. Hibbert	c Tolchard b Old	6	not out	16
D.F. Whatmore	c Edmonds b Lever	27		
G.N. Yallop	b Edmonds	10		
P. Melville	c Edmonds b Emburey	16		
J.K. Moss	c Emburey b Edmonds	73		
T.J. Laughlin	run out	37		
I.L. Maddocks	c Radley b Edmonds	8		
I.W. Callen	c Tolchard b Emburey	8		
A. Hurst	b Emburey	1		
J.D. Higgs	not out	1		
	lb 15 nb 4	19		
	Total	254	Total (0 wkts)	33

Bowling									
Old	17	5	44	1	Lever	4	1	3	0
Lever	18	3	52	2	Emburey	5	0	11	0
Hendrick	11	2	29	0	Edmonds	2	0	3	0
Edmonds	22	6	48	3	Randall	2	0	9	0
Emburey	26.5	5	56	3	Radley	1	0	4	0
Gooch	2	0	6	0					

England XI	*(First Innings)*	
J.M. Brearley	not out	116
G.A. Gooch	lbw b Hurst	3
D.W. Randall	b Wiener	63
D.I. Gower	c & b Wiener	13
C.T. Radley	c & b Higgs	22
R.W. Tolchard	c Whatmore b Higgs	0
P.H. Edmonds	c Melville b Higgs	5
C.M. Old	c Maddocks b Hurst	4
J.E. Emburey	c Higgs b Laughlin	5
J.K. Lever		
M. Hendrick		
	lb 3 w 2 nb 5	10
	Total (8 wkts decl)	241

Bowling				
Hurst	17	4	44	2
Callen	16	4	44	0
Higgs	39	8	82	3
Laughlin	15.7	5	24	1
Wiener	13	3	31	2
Yallop	2	0	6	0

Match drawn

FIFTH MATCH v. CAPITAL TERRITORY AT CANBERRA

England XI				Capital Territory		
G. Boycott	not out		123	A. Irvine	c Hendrick b Willis	0
G.A. Gooch	c Willett b Horneman		13	N. Grant	c Boycott b Willis	2
R.W. Tolchard	c Moore b Samuels		108	G. Hannigan	c Tolchard b Willis	0
D.W. Randall	not out		0	W. Robson	c Gooch b Willis	1
D.I. Gower				K. Owen	c Boycott b Hendrick	3
J.M. Brearley				S. Bray	c Lever b Embury	12
G. Miller				B. Willett	c Randall b Hendrick	32
J.E. Emburey				G. Samuels	c Miller b Emburey	16
J.K. Lever				D. Moore	c Lever b Miller	1
R.G.D. Willis				P. Horneman	c & b Miller	0
M. Hendrick				A. Macdonald	not out	0
	b 2 lb 7 nb 2		11			
	Total (2 wkts, 40 overs)		255		Total (33.6 overs)	76

Bowling

Capital Territory					*England*				
Horneman	8	2	15	1	Willis	8	3	10	4
Macdonald	8	0	44	0	Hendrick	7	3	7	2
Owen	3	0	29	0	Miller	4.6	1	5	2
Grant	5	0	52	0	Lever	8	0	27	0
Moore	8	0	46	0	Emburey	6	0	18	2
Samuels	8	0	58	1					

England won by 179 runs

SIXTH MATCH v. NEW SOUTH WALES AT SYDNEY

England XI	*(First Innings)*			*(Second Innings)*	
G. Boycott	c Border b Lawson	14		not out	4
G.A. Gooch	c Rixon b Border	66		not out	0
D.W. Randall	c Hughes b Clews	110			
C.T. Radley	c Hughes b Border	13			
D.I. Gower	b Hourn	26			
G. Miller	st Rixon b Hourn	5			
I.T. Botham	c Toohey b Clews	56			
R.W. Taylor	c Hilditch b Lawson	9			
J.E. Emburey	c Johnston b Lawson	0			
R.G.D. Willis	not out	21			
M. Hendrick	b Border	20			
	b 17 lb 6 w 2 nb 9	34			
	Total	374		Total (0 wkts)	4

Bowling

Lawson	17	5	39	3	Lawson	0.5	0	4	0
Watson	18	2	61	0					
Clews	13	1	88	2					
Hourn	32	4	114	2					
Border	12.1	2	38	3					

New South Wales	(First Innings)		(Second Innings)	
J. Dyson	c Boycott b Miller	67	c Gooch b Willis	6
A.M. Hilditch	c Taylor b Willis	4	b Botham	93
P.M. Toohey	c Gower b Hendrick	23	c Gooch b Botham	20
A.R. Border	c Taylor b Miller	11	c Taylor b Botham	12
D.A.H. Johnston	c Hendrick b Miller	16	c Gooch b Botham	3
G.C. Hughes	c Hendrick b Miller	27	b Emburey	11
M.L. Clews	st Taylor b Emburey	1	run out	5
S.L. Rixon	c Hendrick b Miller	10	c Botham b Emburey	24
G.G. Watson	c Boycott b Emburey	2	not out	14
G.F. Lawson	not out	0	c Miller b Willis	7
D.W. Hourn	c Emburey b Miller	0	b Botham	0
	lb 1 nb 3	4	b 6 lb 4 w 1 nb 4	15
	Total	165	Total	210

Bowling

Willis	8	3	16	1	Willis	15	3	39	2
Hendrick	12	2	33	1	Botham	17.2	6	51	5
Botham	9	2	41	0	Hendrick	4	2	4	0
Miller	18.4	3	56	6	Emburey	22	5	44	2
Emburey	10	4	15	2	Miller	24	6	56	0
					Gooch	1	0	1	0

England won by 10 wickets

SEVENTH MATCH v. QUEENSLAND COUNTRY XI AT BUNDABERG

England XI			Queensland Country XI		
J.M. Brearley	c Ziebell b Stewart	59	S.N. Ledger	ret. hurt	8
G. Miller	c Hartley b Wilkinson	3	K. Maher	b Miller	47
C.T. Radley	c Hartley b Brabon	16	P. Ledger	c Tolchard b Lever	4
R.W. Tolchard	c Maher b Carlson	74	P.H. Carlson	c Gooch b Miller	31
I.T. Botham	lbw b Wilkinson	22	K.P. Ziebell	c Tolchard b Hendrick	7
D.W. Randall	not out	37	P. Donovan	c Radley b Edmonds	6
G.A. Gooch	not out	32	B. Hartley	b Lever	6
J.K. Lever			G. Bell	lbw b Edmonds	5
P.H. Edmonds			G. Stewart	not out	0
J.E. Emburey			R. Wilkinson	c Tolchard b Lever	1
M. Hendrick			G. Brabon	c Tolchard b Lever	0
	lb 7 w 4 nb 5	16		lb 2 nb 10	12
	Total (5 wkts, 35 overs)	259		Total (31.6 overs)	127

Bowling
Queensland Country

Brabon	7	0	33	1	*England*				
Wilkinson	7	0	47	2	Botham	7	0	34	0
Bell	7	1	68	0	Lever	5.6	1	17	4
Carlson	7	0	34	1	Emburey	4	1	15	0
Stewart	7	0	61	1	Hendrick	7	0	28	1
					Miller	4	1	15	2
					Edmonds	4	1	6	2

England won by 132 runs

EIGHTH MATCH v. QUEENSLAND AT BRISBANE

Queensland	(First Innings)		(Second Innings)	
M.J. Walters	c Gower b Willis	0	ret. hurt	4
W.R. Broad	c Taylor b Old	41	lbw b Willis	0
A.D. Ogilvie	ret. hurt	43	(7) c Gower b Willis	45
G.J. Cosier	c Taylor b Botham	32	(3) b Willis	0
P.H. Carlson	c Miller b Old	1	(4) b Botham	37
T.V. Hohns	c Taylor b Willis	3	(5) c Old b Botham	43
J.A. Maclean	c Boycott b Botham	1	c Gooch b Old	94
G.K. Whyte	c Brearley b Old	10	(6) b Botham	0
G. Dymock	c Brearley b Botham	13	c Taylor b Botham	16
L.F. Balcom	not out	10	b Botham	21
G.W. Brabon	b Old	2	not out	2
	nb 16	16	b 4 lb 2 nb 21	27
	Total	172	Total	289

Bowling									
Willis	11	1	40	2	Willis	11	1	46	3
Old	14.7	4	33	4	Old	14.2	3	63	1
Botham	12	1	66	3	Botham	20	3	70	5
Gooch	3	0	11	0	Miller	11	1	40	0
Edmonds	5	2	6	0	Edmonds	8	1	35	0
					Gooch	1	0	8	0

England XI	(First Innings)		(Second Innings)	
G. Boycott	c Cosier b Brabon	6	c Maclean b Balcom	60
G.A. Gooch	c Brabon b Dymock	34	c Ogilvie b Carlson	22
D.W. Randall	c Maclean b Balcom	66	b Whyte	47
R.W. Taylor	c Maclean b Dymock	2		
J.M. Brearley	not out	75	(4) not out	38
D.I. Gower	b Balcom	6	(5) c Cosier b Hohns	1
G. Miller	c Maclean b Dymock	18	(6) not out	22
I.T. Botham	c Maclean b Dymock	6		
C.M. Old	lbw b Balcom	2		
P.H. Edmonds	c Maclean b Cosier	14		
R.G.D. Willis	b Brabon	6		
	b 1 lb 3 w 1 nb 14	19	b 7 lb 2 nb 9	18
	Total	254	Total	208

Bowling									
Balcom	13	1	56	3	Balcom	12	2	25	1
Brabon	10.1	1	45	2	Brabon	5	0	31	0
Carlson	14	1	48	0	Carlson	9.3	1	29	1
Dymock	19	3	46	4	Dymock	17	5	38	0
Hohns	2	0	3	0	Cosier	5	2	10	0
Cosier	4	0	19	1	Whyte	15	3	44	1
Whyte	7	3	18	0	Hohns	8	5	13	1

England won by 6 wickets

NINTH MATCH: FIRST TEST MATCH — AUSTRALIA v. ENGLAND AT BRISBANE

Australia	*(First Innings)*		*(Second Innings)*	
G.M. Wood	c Taylor b Old	7	(2) lbw b Old	19
G.J. Cosier	run out	1	(1) b Willis	0
P.M. Toohey	b Willis	1	lbw b Botham	1
G.N. Yallop	c Gooch b Willis	7	c & b Willis	102
K.J. Hughes	c Taylor b Botham	4	c Edmonds b Willis	129
T.J. Laughlin	c Sub b Willis	2	lbw b Old	5
J.A. Maclean	not out	33	lbw b Miller	15
B. Yardley	c Taylor b Willis	17	c Brearley b Miller	16
R.M. Hogg	c Taylor b Botham	36	b Botham	16
A.G. Hurst	c Taylor b Botham	0	b Botham	0
J.D. Higgs	b Old	1	not out	0
	lb 1 nb 6	7	b 9 lb 5 nb 22	36
	Total	116	Total	339

Bowling									
Willis	14	2	44	4	Willis	27.6	3	69	3
Old	9.7	1	24	2	Old	17	1	60	2
Botham	12	1	40	3	Botham	26	5	95	3
Gooch	1	0	1	0					
Edmonds	1	1	0	0	Edmonds	12	1	27	0
					Miller	34	12	52	2

England	*(First Innings)*		*(Second Innings)*	
G. Boycott	c Hughes b Hogg	13	run out	16
G.A. Gooch	c Laughlin b Hogg	2	c Yardley b Hogg	2
D.W. Randall	c Laughlin b Hurst	75	not out	74
R.W. Taylor	lbw b Hurst	20		
J.M. Brearley	c Maclean b Hogg	6	(4) c Maclean b Hogg	13
D.I. Gower	c Maclean b Hurst	44	(5) not out	48
I.T. Botham	c Maclean b Hogg	49		
G. Miller	lbw b Hogg	27		
P.H. Edmonds	c Maclean b Hogg	1		
C.M. Old	not out	29		
R.G.D. Willis	c Maclean b Hurst	8		
	b 7 lb 4 nb 1	12	b 12 lb 3 nb 2	17
	Total	286	Total (3 wkts)	170

Bowling									
Hurst	27.4	6	93	4	Hurst	10	4	17	0
Hogg	28	8	74	6	Hogg	12.5	2	35	1
Laughlin	22	6	54	0	Laughlin	3	0	6	0
Yardley	7	1	34	0	Yardley	13	1	41	1
Cosier	5	1	10	0	Cosier	3	0	11	0
Higgs	6	2	9	0	Higgs	12	1	43	0

England won by 7 wickets

TENTH MATCH v. WESTERN AUSTRALIA AT PERTH

England XI	(First Innings)		(Second Innings)	
G. Boycott	lbw b Clark	4	c Marsh b Yardley	13
G.A. Gooch	c Wright b Alderman	3	c Wright b Porter	15
C.T. Radley	b Alderman	2	c Marsh b Yardley	18
J.M. Brearley	c Wright b Porter	11	b Yardley	18
D.I. Gower	c Wright b Alderman	0	c Marsh b Porter	4
R.W. Tolchard	not out	61	b Yardley	3
I.T. Botham	c Charlesworth b Porter	4	c Marsh b Yardley	4
P.H. Edmonds	lbw b Porter	21	c Wright b Alderman	27
J.E. Emburey	c Wright b Clark	22	not out	7
J.K. Lever	c Wright b Mann	2	b Alderman	1
M. Hendrick	c Charlesworth b Mann	6	b Clark	8
	b 1 lb 2 nb 4 w 1	8	b 7 nb 1	8
	Total	144	Total	126

Bowling

Alderman	12	4	18	3	Alderman	9	2	26	2
Clark	16	4	50	2	Clark	12	2	22	1
Porter	17	4	37	3	Porter	16	9	16	2
Yardley	2	0	7	0	Yardley	13	1	54	5
Mann	8.3	2	24	2					

Western Australia	(First Innings)		(Second Innings)	
G.M. Wood	b Lever	2	lbw b Botham	15
R.I. Charlesworth	c Tolchard b Botham	3	lbw b Lever	6
K.J. Hughes	b Botham	8	lbw b Botham	1
G.J. Marsh	c Tolchard b Botham	9	c Tolchard b Hendrick	9
R.J. Inverarity	c Tolchard b Hendrick	0	lbw b Botham	2
A.L. Mann	c Botham b Hendrick	3	c Tolchard b Botham	0
G.D. Porter	c Brearley b Hendrick	8	c Tolchard b Hendrick	2
B. Yardley	c Tolchard b Hendrick	8	not out	38
K.J. Wright	c Brearley b Botham	0	b Hendrick	0
W.M. Clark	not out	2	run out	1
T.M. Alderman	c Botham b Hendrick	1	run out	2
	lb 3 w 1 nb 4	8	lb 2	2
	Total	52	Total	78

Bowling

Lever	8	3	10	1	Lever	7	3	16	1
Botham	9	3	16	4	Botham	13.5	4	37	4
Hendrick	5.4	2	11	5	Hendrick	7	2	23	3
Gooch	2	0	7	0					

England won by 140 runs

ELEVENTH MATCH v. WESTERN AUSTRALIAN COUNTRY XI AT ALBANY

England XI			W. Australian Country XI		
G. Boycott	run out	29	S. Fyfe	lbw b Edmonds	3
G.A. Gooch	run out	112	R. Miguel	c Old b Edmonds	53
D.W. Randall	c McCormack b Ditchburn	10	K. Macleay	c Randall b Miller	13
G. Miller	c & b Draper	8	T. Waldron	b Miller	25
R.W. Tolchard	not out	26	G. Hogg	c Randall b Miller	0
C.T. Radley	not out	20	J. McCormack	c Gooch b Edmonds	2
P.H. Edmonds			G. Willey	c Gooch b Edmonds	3
R.W. Taylor			R. Ditchburn	b Miller	31
C.M. Old			W. Sounness	c Tolchard b Edmonds	0
J.K. Lever			G. Rose	c Radley b Edmonds	1
J.E. Emburey			K. Draper	not out	0
	Extras	3		b 1 lb 6 nb 1	8
	Total (4 wkts, 40 overs)	208		Total (34.3 overs)	139

Bowling

Western Australian Country						*England*				
Draper	12	2	52	1		Lever	3	0	7	0
Willey	7	0	20	0		Old	3	0	3	0
Ditchburn	8	0	64	1		Edmonds	14.3	1	53	6
Macleay	6	0	28	0		Miller	14	1	68	4
Sounness	3	0	19	0						
Rose	4	0	22	0						

England won by 69 runs

TWELFTH MATCH: SECOND TEST MATCH – AUSTRALIA v. ENGLAND AT PERTH

England	*(First Innings)*		*(Second Innings)*	
G. Boycott	lbw b Hurst	77	lbw b Hogg	23
G.A. Gooch	c Maclean b Hogg	1	lbw b Hogg	43
D.W. Randall	c Wood b Hogg	0	c Cosier b Yardley	45
J.M. Brearley	c Maclean b Dymock	17	c Maclean b Hogg	0
D.I. Gower	b Hogg	102	c Maclean b Hogg	12
I.T. Botham	lbw b Hurst	11	c Wood b Yardley	30
G. Miller	b Hogg	40	c Toohey b Yardley	25
R.W. Taylor	c Hurst b Yardley	12	(9) c Maclean b Hogg	2
J.K. Lever	c Cosier b Hurst	14	(8) c Maclean b Hurst	10
R.G.D. Willis	c Yallop b Hogg	2	not out	3
M. Hendrick	not out	7	b Dymock	1
	b 6 lb 9 w 3 nb 8	26	lb 6 nb 8	14
	Total	309	Total	208

Bowling

Hogg	30.5	9	65	5	Hogg	17	2	57	5
Dymock	34	4	72	1	Dymock	16.3	2	53	1
Hurst	26	7	70	3	Hurst	17	5	43	1
Yardley	23	1	62	1	Yardley	16	1	41	3
Cosier	4	2	14	0					

Australia	(First Innings)		(Second Innings)	
G.M. Wood	lbw b Lever	5	c Taylor b Lever	64
W.M. Darling	run out	25	c Boycott b Lever	5
K.J. Hughes	b Willis	16	c Gooch b Willis	12
G.N. Yallop	b Willis	3	c Taylor b Hendrick	3
P.M. Toohey	not out	81	c Taylor b Hendrick	0
G.J. Cosier	c Gooch b Willis	4	lbw b Miller	47
J.A. McLean	c Gooch b Miller	0	c Brearley b Miller	1
B. Yardley	c Taylor b Hendrick	12	c Botham b Lever	7
R.M. Hogg	c Taylor b Willis	18	b Miller	0
G. Dymock	b Hendrick	11	not out	6
A.G. Hurst	c Taylor b Willis	5	b Lever	5
	lb 7 w 1 nb 2	10	lb 3 nb 4 w 4	11
	Total	190	Total	161

Bowling									
Lever	7	0	20	1	Lever	8.1	2	28	4
Botham	11	2	46	0	Botham	11	1	54	0
Willis	18.5	5	44	5	Willis	12	1	36	1
Hendrick	14	1	39	2	Hendrick	8	3	11	2
Miller	16	6	31	1	Miller	7	4	21	3

England won by 166 runs

THIRTEENTH MATCH v. SOUTH AUSTRALIA AT ADELAIDE

South Australia	(First Innings)		(Second Innings)	
J. Nash	c Tolchard b Old	10	lbw b Emburey	25
W.M. Darling	c Tolchard b Old	19	(7) not out	41
I.R. McLean	c Tolchard b Gooch	7	(2) c & b Emburey	25
B.L. Causby	b Old	87	(3) c Randall b Emburey	7
R. Parker	c & b Edmonds	51	(4) c Randall b Emburey	42
R.K. Blewett	c Old b Emburey	19	c Brearley b Emburey	51
P.R. Sleep	not out	31	(5) c Taylor b Old	18
S. Gentle	lbw b Lever	1	not out	21
A.T. Sincock	not out	12		
G.R. Attenborough				
D. Johnston	lb 3 nb 1	4	lb 1	1
	Total (7 wkts decl)	241	Total (6 wkts decl)	231

Bowling									
Lever	16	1	63	1	Lever	10	1	33	0
Old	18	2	55	3	Gooch	4	0	11	0
Gooch	6	1	16	1	Emburey	26	3	67	5
Emburey	17	3	48	1	Edmonds	28	9	91	0
Edmonds	17	3	55	1	Miller	4	1	6	0
					Old	5	0	21	1
					Boycott	1	0	1	0

England	*(First Innings)*		*(Second Innings)*	
G. Boycott	c Gentle b Sincock	4	(11) not out	7
G.A. Gooch	c Gentle b Causby	20	(5) st Gentle b Blewett	64
C.T. Radley	c Gentle b Attenborough	60	lbw b Attenborough	1
R.W. Tolchard	run out	72	lbw b Johnston	6
D.W. Randall	c Gentle b Attenborough	47	(2) c Blewett b Johnston	45
J.M. Brearley	not out	18	(1) c Parker b Johnston	26
G. Miller	not out	2	(6) not out	68
C.M. Old			(7) b Attenborough	2
P.H. Edmonds			(8) lbw b Blewett	2
J.E. Emburey			(9) b Blewett	0
J.K. Lever			(10) c Darling b Attenborough	11
	b 3 lb 4 nb 4	11	b 1 lb 2 nb 3	6
	Total (5 wkts decl)	234	Total (9 wkts)	238

Bowling

Attenborough	13	5	41	2	Sincock	5	0	39	0
Johnston	8	2	21	0	Attenborough	16	1	92	3
Sincock	5	0	27	1	Johnston	7	0	44	3
Causby	6	0	34	1	Sleep	2	0	22	0
Sleep	12	1	58	0	Blewett	7	0	35	3
Blewett	8	1	41	0					
Nash	1	0	1	0					

Match drawn

FOURTEENTH MATCH: AUSTRALIA v. ENGLAND ONE-DAY INTERNATIONAL AT MELBOURNE

No match – abandoned because of rain

FIFTEENTH MATCH: THIRD TEST MATCH — AUSTRALIA v. ENGLAND AT MELBOURNE

Australia	*(First Innings)*		*(Second Innings)*	
G.M. Wood	c Emburey b Miller	100	b Botham	34
W.M. Darling	run out	33	c Randall b Miller	21
K.J. Hughes	c Taylor b Botham	0	c Gower b Botham	48
G.N. Yallop	c Hendrick b Botham	41	c Taylor b Miller	16
P.M. Toohey	c Randall b Miller	32	c Botham b Emburey	20
A.R. Border	c Brearley b Hendrick	29	run out	0
J.A. Maclean	b Botham	8	c Hendrick b Emburey	10
R.M. Hogg	c Randall b Miller	0	b Botham	1
G. Dymock	b Hendrick	0	c Brearley b Hendrick	6
A.G. Hurst	b Hendrick	0	(11) not out	0
J.D. Higgs	not out	1	(10) st Taylor b Emburey	0
	lb 8 nb 6	14	b 4 lb 6 nb 1	11
	Total	258	Total	167

Bowling

Willis	13	2	47	0	Willis	7	0	21	0
Botham	20.1	4	68	3	Botham	15	4	41	3
Hendrick	23	3	50	3	Hendrick	14	4	25	1
Emburey	14	1	44	0	Emburey	21.2	12	30	3
Miller	19	6	35	3	Miller	14	5	39	2

England	*(First Innings)*				*(Second Innings)*				
G. Boycott	b Hogg			1	lbw b Hurst				38
J.M. Brearley	lbw b Hogg			1	c Maclean b Dymock				0
D.W. Randall	lbw b Hurst			13	lbw b Hogg				2
G.A. Gooch	c Border b Dymock			25	lbw b Hogg				40
D.I. Gower	lbw b Dymock			29	lbw b Dymock				49
I.T. Botham	c Darling b Higgs			22	c Maclean b Higgs				10
G. Miller	b Hogg			7	c Hughes b Higgs				1
R.W. Taylor	b Hogg			1	c Maclean b Hogg				5
J.E. Emburey	b Hogg			0	not out				7
R.G.D. Willis	c Darling b Dymock			19	c Yallop b Hogg				3
M. Hendrick	not out			6	b Hogg				0
	Extras			19	b 10 lb 7 nb 6 w 1				24
	Total			143	Total				179

Bowling									
Hogg	17	7	30	5	Hogg	17	5	36	5
Hurst	12	2	24	1	Hurst	11	1	39	1
Dymock	15.6	4	38	3	Dymock	18	4	37	2
Higgs	19	9	32	1	Higgs	16	2	29	2
					Border	5	0	14	0

Australia won by 103 runs

SIXTEENTH MATCH: FOURTH TEST MATCH — AUSTRALIA v. ENGLAND AT SYDNEY

England	*(First Innings)*				*(Second Innings)*				
G. Boycott	c Border b Hurst			8	lbw b Hogg				0
J.M. Brearley	b Hogg			17	b Border				53
D.W. Randall	c Wood b Hurst			0	lbw b Hogg				150
G.A. Gooch	c Toohey b Higgs			18	c Wood b Higgs				22
D.I. Gower	c Maclean b Hurst			7	c Maclean b Hogg				34
I.T. Botham	c Yallop b Hogg			59	c Wood b Higgs				6
G. Miller	c Maclean b Hurst			4	lbw b Hogg				17
R.W. Taylor	c Border b Higgs			10	not out				21
J.E. Emburey	c Wood b Higgs			0	c Darling b Higgs				14
R.G.D. Willis	not out			7	c Toohey b Higgs				0
M. Hendrick	b Hurst			10	c Toohey b Higgs				7
	b 1 lb 1 w 2 nb 8			12	b 5 lb 3 nb 14				22
	Total			152	Total				346

Bowling									
Hogg	11	3	36	2	Hogg	28	10	67	4
Dymock	13	1	34	0	Dymock	17	4	35	0
Hurst	10.6	2	28	5	Hurst	19	3	43	0
Higgs	18	4	42	3	Higgs	59.6	15	148	5
Border					Border	23	11	31	1

Australia	(First Innings)		(Second Innings)	
G.M. Wood	b Willis	0	run out	27
W.M. Darling	c Botham b Miller	91	c Gooch b Hendrick	13
K.J. Hughes	c Emburey b Willis	48	c Emburey b Miller	15
G.N. Yallop	c Botham b Hendrick	44	c & b Hendrick	1
P.M. Toohey	c Gooch b Botham	1	b Miller	5
A.R. Border	not out	60	not out	45
J.A. Maclean	lbw b Emburey	12	c Botham b Miller	0
R.M. Hogg	run out	6	(9) c Botham b Emburey	0
G. Dymock	b Botham	5	(8) b Emburey	0
J.D. Higgs	c Botham b Hendrick	11	lbw b Emburey	3
A.G. Hurst	run out	0	b Emburey	0
	b 2 lb 3 nb 11	16	lb 1 nb 1	2
	Total	294	Total	111

Bowling									
Willis	9	2	33	2	Willis	2	0	8	0
Botham	28	3	87	2					
Hendrick	24	4	50	2	Hendrick	10	3	17	2
Miller	13	2	37	1	Miller	20	7	38	3
Emburey	29	10	57	1	Emburey	17.2	7	46	4
Gooch	5	1	14	0					

England won by 93 runs

SEVENTEENTH MATCH: AUSTRALIA v. ENGLAND SECOND ONE-DAY INTERNATIONAL AT SYDNEY

Australia		
W.M. Darling	not out	7
G.M. Wood	c Tolchard b Old	6
K.J. Hughes	not out	0
	Extras	4
	Total (1 wkt)	17

EIGHTEENTH MATCH v. NORTHERN NEW SOUTH WALES AT NEWCASTLE

Northern New South Wales	(First Innings)		(Second Innings)	
J. Hogg	lbw b Old	5	c Gooch b Lever	4
J. Gardner	c Randall b Miller	59	b Lever	8
C. Evans	c & b Gooch	0	(4) lbw b Old	64
R. Neal	c Gooch b Edmonds	11	(3) lbw b Edmonds	44
C. Beatty	c Brearley b Boycott	62	c Gooch b Lever	12
M. Hill	c & b Edmonds	7	(7) lbw b Old	5
K. Thompson	run out	12	(8) lbw b Edmonds	0
J. Hill	c & b Edmonds	34	(6) b Edmonds	0
R. Holland	b Boycott	3	b Old	1
G. Davis	not out	11	not out	13
G. Sneesby	c Gooch b Old	2	c Gooch b Old	2
	b 3 lb 13 nb 1	17		
	Total (9 wkts decl)	223	Total	166

Bowling									
Old	11	4	18	2	Old	13	2	30	4
Lever	14	3	54	0	Lever	8	1	24	3
Gooch	4	2	11	1	Edmonds	22	4	49	3
Edmonds	18.4	1	66	3	Emburey	7	1	23	0
Miller	7	0	32	1	Miller	5	0	23	0
Boycott	2	0	9	2	Boycott	2	0	4	0
Emburey	4	0	16	0					

England XI	*(First Innings)*		*(Second Innings)*	
G. Boycott	c Thompson b Sneesby	15	not out	117
J.M. Brearley	b M. Hill	66	c Holland b M. Hill	50
C.T. Radley	c & b M. Hill	0	not out	55
R.W. Tolchard	hit wkt b Davies	2		
G.A. Gooch	c Holland b M. Hill	1		
D.W. Randall	b Davis	1		
G. Miller	b Holland	11		
P.H. Edmonds	lbw b Holland	10		
C.M. Old	b Holland	1		
J.E. Emburey	not out	26		
J.K. Lever	c Thompson b Holland	27		
	Total	163	Total (1 wkt)	230

Bowling

Davis	11	4	24	2		Davis	13	0	46	0
Sneesby	7	0	27	1		Sneesby	6	1	19	0
Holland	14.7	1	60	4		Holland	18	1	75	0
M. Hill	14	2	49	3		M. Hill	17	8	41	1
						J. Hill	6	1	10	0
						Neal	2	0	21	0
						Beatty	1	0	10	0

England won by 9 wickets

NINETEENTH MATCH v. TASMANIA AT LAUNCESTON

England XI			**Tasmania**		
G. Boycott	b Scholes	13	S.J. Howard	c Taylor b Willis	10
G. Miller	b Cowmeadow	0	G. Goodman	c Botham b Edmonds	11
C.T. Radley	run out	44	M.J. Sellers	run out	2
D.W. Randall	b Cowmeadow	60	T.W. Docking	c Taylor b Hendrick	12
D.I. Gower	run out	17	R.D. Woolley	run out	7
I.T. Botham	c Boon b Wilson	61	D.A. Boon	c Boycott b Edmonds	15
P.H. Edmonds	not out	26	J. Simmons	b Botham	4
R.W. Taylor	b Wilson	12	G.J. Cowmeadow	b Miller	0
J.K. Lever	run out	1	J.A. Wilson	not out	9
M. Hendrick			M.J. Scholes	c sub b Miller	1
R.G.D. Willis			G.R. Whitney	c & b Miller	0
	Extras	6		Extras	6
	Total (8 wkts, 40 overs)	240		Total (34.4 overs)	77

Bowling

Tasmania						*England*				
Cowmeadow	8	1	46	2		Willis	6	1	8	1
Wilson	8	1	36	2		Lever	3	1	9	0
Whitney	8	0	73	0		Hendrick	8	2	17	1
Scholes	8	0	40	1		Edmonds	8	4	16	2
Simmons	8	0	39	0		Botham	6	0	18	1
						Miller	3.4	1	3	3

England won by 163 runs

TWENTIETH MATCH v. TASMANIA AT HOBART

Tasmania	*(First Innings)*		*(Second Innings)*	
M.J. Norman	c Taylor b Old	13	b Emburey	43
G. Goodman	c Taylor b Old	1	c Taylor b Willis	1
S.J. Howard	c Taylor b Old	13	b Lever	20
J.H. Hampshire	c Taylor b Old	0	not out	46
R. Woolley	b Old	4	c Radley b Miller	0
T.J. Docking	b Emburey	39	not out	2
J. Simmons	c Miller b Old	1		
D.J. Gatenby	b Willis	1		
G.J. Cowmeadow	c Edmonds b Willis	10		
M.B. Scholes	b Miller	10		
G.R. Whitney	not out	0		
	b 5 lb 3 nb 5	13	b 2 lb 1 nb 3	6
	Total	105	Total (4 wkts)	118

Bowling									
Willis	10	1	24	2	Willis	4	1	9	1
Old	14	3	42	6	Old	5	2	12	0
Lever	7	3	18	0	Lever	9	0	27	1
Emburey	4	3	1	1	Edmonds	10	3	27	0
Miller	3	1	7	1	Emburey	6	1	15	1
					Miller	5	1	18	1
					Boycott	1	0	4	0

England XI		
G. Boycott	not out	90
G.A. Gooch	c Goodman b Whitney	14
C.T. Radley	c Woolley b Cowmeadow	15
D.I. Gower	b Gatenby	30
R.W. Taylor	b Whitney	1
G. Miller	b Gatenby	44
P.H. Edmonds	not out	7
C.M. Old		
J.E. Emburey		
J.K. Lever		
R.G.D. Willis		
	b 4 lb 2 nb 3	9
	Total (5 wkts decl)	210

Bowling				
Cowmeadow	16	2	64	1
Whitney	26	3	73	2
Scholes	10	4	40	0
Gatenby	5	1	22	2
Simmons	1	0	2	0

Match drawn

TWENTY-FIRST MATCH: AUSTRALIA v. ENGLAND ONE-DAY INTERNATIONAL AT MELBOURNE

Australia			England		
G.M. Wood	c Gower b Edmonds	28	G. Boycott	not out	39
A.M. Hilditch	c Bairstow b Botham	10	J.M. Brearley	b Hogg	0
A.R. Border	c Willis b Hendrick	11	D.W. Randall	c Yallop b Dymock	12
G.N. Yallop	run out	9	G.A. Gooch	b Carlson	23
K.J. Hughes	lbw b Hendrick	0	D.I. Gower	not out	19
P.H. Carlson	c Randall b Willis	11	I.T. Botham		
T.J. Laughlin	c Willis b Hendrick	6	D. Bairstow		
J.A. Maclean	c Edmonds b Botham	11	P.H. Edmonds		
R.M. Hogg	c Botham b Hendrick	4	J.K. Lever		
G. Dymock	c & b Botham	1	R.G.D. Willis		
A.G. Hurst	not out	0	M. Hendrick		
	b 4 lb 2 nb 4	10		lb 5 nb 4	9
	Total			Total	
	(33.5 overs)	101		(3 wkts, 28.2 overs)	102

Bowling

England					Australia				
Willis	8	4	15	1	Hogg	6	1	20	1
Lever	5	2	7	0	Dymock	6	1	16	1
Hendrick	8	1	25	4	Laughlin	5	1	13	0
Botham	4.5	2	16	3	Carlson	5	0	21	1
Edmonds	7	0	26	1	Hurst	5.2	1	14	0
Gooch	1	0	2	0	Border	1	0	9	0

England won by 7 wkts

TWENTY-SECOND MATCH: FIFTH TEST MATCH — AUSTRALIA v. ENGLAND AT ADELAIDE

England	*(First Innings)*		*(Second Innings)*	
G. Boycott	c Wright b Hurst	6	c Hughes b Hurst	49
J.M. Brearley	c Wright b Hogg	2	lbw b Carlson	9
D.W. Randall	c Carlson b Hurst	4	c Yardley b Hurst	15
G.A. Gooch	c Hughes b Hogg	1	b Carlson	18
D.I. Gower	lbw b Hurst	9	lbw b Higgs	21
I.T. Botham	st Wright b Higgs	74	c Yardley b Hurst	7
G. Miller	lbw b Hogg	31	c Wright b Hurst	64
R.W. Taylor	run out	4	c Wright b Hogg	97
J.E. Emburey	b Higgs	4	b Hogg	42
R.G.D. Willis	c Darling b Hogg	24	c Wright b Hogg	12
M. Hendrick	not out	0	not out	3
	b 1 lb 4 nb 2 w 3	10	b 1 lb 16 nb 4 w 2	23
	Total	169	Total	360

Bowling

Hogg	10.4	1	26	4	Hogg	27.6	7	59	3
Hurst	14	1	65	3	Hurst	37	9	97	4
Carlson	9	1	34	0	Carlson	27	8	41	2
Yardley	4	0	25	0	Yardley	20	6	60	0
Higgs	3	1	9	2	Higgs	28	4	75	1
					Border	3	2	5	0

Australia	(First Innings)		(Second Innings)	
W.M. Darling	c Willis b Botham	15	b Botham	18
G.M. Wood	c Randall b Emburey	35	run out	9
K.J. Hughes	c Emburey b Hendrick	4	c Gower b Hendrick	46
G.N. Yallop	b Hendrick	0	b Hendrick	36
A.R. Border	c Taylor b Botham	11	b Willis	1
P.H. Carlson	c Taylor b Botham	0	c Gower b Hendrick	21
B. Yardley	b Botham	28	c Brearley b Willis	0
K.J. Wright	lbw b Emburey	29	c Emburey b Miller	0
R.M. Hogg	b Willis	0	b Miller	2
J.D. Higgs	run out	16	not out	3
A.G. Hurst	not out	17	b Willis	13
	b 1 lb 3 nb 5	9	lb 1 nb 10	11
	Total	164	Total	160

Bowling

Willis	11	1	55	1	Willis	12	3	41	3
Hendrick	19	1	45	2	Hendrick	14	6	19	3
Botham	11.4	0	42	4	Botham	14	4	37	1
Emburey	12	7	13	2	Emburey	9	5	16	0
					Miller	18	3	36	2

England won by 205 runs

TWENTY-THIRD MATCH v. TASMANIA AT MELBOURNE

Tasmania			England XI		
M. Norman	c Bairstow b Willis	0	G. Boycott	c Simmons b Sherriff	1
G. Goodman	c Willis b Old	36	G.A. Gooch	lbw b Simmons	29
D.J. Smith	c Willis b Edmonds	25	C.T. Radley	b Cowmeadow	6
J.H. Hampshire	c Randall b Old	14	D.W. Randall	b Wilson	22
D. Boon	c Randall b Emburey	8	D.I. Gower	c Woolley b Cowmeadow	20
T. Docking	c Bairstow b Willis	17	D.L. Bairstow	b Sherriff	17
R.D. Woolley	not out	11	P.H. Edmonds	not out	14
J. Simmons	not out	6	C.M. Old	c Woolley b Wilson	3
G.J. Cowmeadow			J.E. Emburey	not out	0
J.A. Wilson			R.G.D. Willis		
R. Sherriff			J.K. Lever		
	lb 13 nb 1	14		b 10 lb 10 nb 2	22
	Total			Total	
	(6 wkts, 48 overs)	131		(7 wkts, 43.4 overs)	134

Bowling

England

Willis	9	3	20	2
Old	10	4	17	2
Lever	9	1	25	0
Edmonds	10	3	18	1
Emburey	10	1	37	1

Tasmania

Cowmeadow	10	2	30	2
Sherriff	10	3	16	3
Wilson	10	3	19	1
Simmons	9	1	23	1
Smith	4	0	20	0
Goodman	0.3	0	4	0

England won by 3 wkts

TWENTY-FOURTH MATCH: AUSTRALIA v. ENGLAND ONE-DAY INTERNATIONAL AT MELBOURNE

England			Australia		
G. Boycott	lbw b Laughlin	33	G.M. Wood	b Old	23
J.M. Brearley	c Wright b Dymock	0	W.M. Darling	c Old b Willis	7
D.W. Randall	lbw b Dymock	4	K.J. Hughes	c Boycott b Lever	50
G.A. Gooch	c Hurst b Carlson	19	G.N. Yallop	c Gower b Hendrick	31
D.I. Gower	not out	101	P.M. Toohey	not out	54
I.T. Botham	c Wood b Hurst	31	G.J. Cosier	b Lever	28
D.L. Bairstow	run out	1	P.H. Carlson	c Boycott b Lever	0
C.M. Old	not out	16	T.J. Laughlin	not out	15
R.G.D. Willis			A.G. Hurst		
J.K. Lever			K.J. Wright		
M. Hendrick			G. Dymock		
	b 3 lb 3 nb 1	7		lb 6 nb 1	7
	Total			Total	
	(6 wkts, 40 overs)	212		(6 wkts, 38.6 overs)	215

Bowling

Australia						*England*				
Hurst	8	1	36	1		Willis	8	1	21	1
Dymock	8	1	31	2		Lever	7	1	51	3
Carlson	8	1	27	1		Hendrick	8	0	47	1
Cosier	8	0	48	0		Old	8	1	31	1
Laughlin	8	0	63	1		Botham	7.6	0	58	0

Australia won by 4 wkts

TWENTY-FIFTH MATCH v. GEELONG AND DISTRICT AT GEELONG

England XI			Geelong and District		
J.M. Brearley	c Ward b Wells	39	C. Lynch	c Taylor b Old	3
D.W. Randall	lbw b Treloar	39	G. Draw	run out	7
C.T. Radley	c & b Wells	0	P. Marshall	b Edmonds	10
G. Miller	c Caulfield b Treloar	5	K. Davis	run out	23
D.I. Gower	c Ward b Caulfield	21	M. Bowtell	run out	0
D.L. Bairstow	c Tory b Caulfield	11	G. Ward	c Gower b Miller	10
P.H. Edmonds	c Tory b Caulfield	5	G. Wells	b Lever	2
C.M. Old	not out	25	P. Caulfield	c Bairstow b Emburey	12
R.W. Taylor	b Tory	4	W. Tory	c Miller b Emburey	5
J.E. Emburey	b McCann	10	T. McCann	not out	10
J.K. Lever			I. Treloar	not out	10
	lb 4 nb 2	6		lb 5 nb 3	8
	Total			Total	
	(9 wkts, 40 overs)	165		(9 wkts, 38.6 overs)	100

Bowling

Geelong						*England*				
McCann	8	1	35	1		Old	6	0	12	1
Caulfield	8	1	28	3		Lever	6	1	18	1
Wells	8	1	38	2		Edmonds	8	1	23	1
Treloar	8	1	26	2		Miller	8	0	22	1
Tory	8	1	32	1		Emburey	8	1	13	2
						Randall	1.6	0	8	0
						Brearley	1	0	4	0

Match abandoned

TWENTY-SIXTH MATCH: AUSTRALIA v. ENGLAND ONE-DAY INTERNATIONAL AT MELBOURNE

England			Australia		
G. Boycott	c Cosier b Dymock	2	G.M. Wood	c Bairstow b Botham	30
J.M. Brearley	c Wright b Cosier	46	W.M. Darling	c Brearley b Willis	14
D.W. Randall	c Hughes b Dymock	0	K.J. Hughes	c Brearley b Willis	0
G.A. Gooch	c Hughes b Hurst	4	G.N. Yallop	b Lever	25
D.I. Gower	c Wood b Hurst	3	P.M. Toohey	not out	16
D.L. Bairstow	run out	3	G.J. Cosier	not out	8
I.T. Botham	b Cosier	13	P.H. Carlson		
P.H. Edmonds	b Laughlin	15	T.J. Laughlin		
J.K. Lever	b Laughlin	1	K.J. Wright		
R.G.D. Willis	c Wright b Cosier	2	G. Dymock		
M. Hendrick	not out	0	A.G. Hurst		
	lb 2 nb 3	5		nb 2	2
	Total			Total	
	(31.7 overs)	94		(4 wkts, 21.5 overs)	95

Bowling

Australia					England				
Hurst	5	3	7	2	Willis	5	2	16	2
Dymock	6	1	21	2	Hendrick	6	0	32	0
Carlson	8	2	22	0	Botham	5.5	0	30	1
Cosier	7	1	22	3	Lever	5	0	15	1
Laughlin	5.7	0	17	2					

Australia won by 6 wkts

TWENTY-SEVENTH MATCH: SIXTH TEST MATCH — AUSTRALIA v. ENGLAND AT SYDNEY

Australia	*(First Innings)*		*(Second Innings)*	
G.M. Wood	c Botham b Hendrick	15	c Willis b Miller	29
A.M. Hilditch	run out	3	c Taylor b Hendrick	1
K.J. Hughes	c Botham b Willis	16	c Gooch b Emburey	7
G.N. Yallop	c Gower b Botham	121	c Taylor b Miller	17
P.M. Toohey	c Taylor b Botham	8	c Gooch b Emburey	0
P.H. Carlson	c Gooch b Botham	2	c Botham b Emburey	0
B. Yardley	b Emburey	7	not out	61
K.J. Wright	st Taylor b Emburey	3	c Boycott b Miller	5
R.M. Hogg	c Emburey b Miller	9	b Miller	7
J.D. Higgs	not out	9	c Botham b Emburey	2
A.G. Hurst	b Botham	0	c & b Miller	4
	lb 3 nb 2	5	b 3 lb 6 nb 1	10
	Total	198	Total	143

Bowling

Willis	11	4	48	1	Willis	3	0	15	0
Hendrick	12	2	21	1	Hendrick	7	3	22	1
Botham	9.7	1	57	4					
Emburey	18	3	48	2	Emburey	24	4	52	4
Miller	9	3	13	1	Miller	27.1	6	44	5
Boycott	1	0	6	0					

England

	(First Innings)		(Second Innings)	
G. Boycott	c Hilditch b Hurst	19	c Hughes b Higgs	13
J.M. Brearley	c Toohey b Higgs	46	not out	20
D.W. Randall	lbw b Hogg	7	not out	0
G.A. Gooch	st Wright b Higgs	74		
D.I. Gower	c Wright b Higgs	65		
I.T. Botham	c Carlson b Yardley	23		
G. Miller	lbw b Hurst	18		
R.W. Taylor	not out	36		
J.E. Emburey	c Hilditch b Hurst	0		
R.G.D. Willis	b Higgs	10		
M. Hendrick	c & b Yardley	0		
	b 3 lb 5 nb 2	10	nb 2	2
	Total (1 wkt)	308	Total	35

Bowling

Hogg	18	6	42	1					
Hurst	20	4	58	3					
Yardley	25	2	105	2	Yardley	5.2	0	21	0
Carlson	10	1	24	0					
Higgs	30	3	69	4	Higgs	5	1	12	1

England won by 9 wkts

TEST AVERAGES

Australia Batting and Fielding

	M	I	NO	R	HS	Avge	100	50	c/s
A.R. Border	3	6	2	146	60*	36.50	0	1	3
G.N. Yallop	6	12	0	391	121	32.58	2	0	3
K.J. Hughes	6	12	0	345	129	28.75	1	0	5
G.M. Wood	6	12	0	344	100	28.67	1	1	6
W.M. Darling	4	8	0	221	91	27.63	0	1	4
B. Yardley	4	8	1	148	61*	21.14	0	1	4
P.M. Toohey	5	10	1	149	81*	16.56	0	1	5
G.J. Cosier	2	4	0	52	47	13.00	0	0	2
J.A. Maclean	4	8	1	79	33*	11.29	0	0	18
K.J. Wright	2	4	0	37	29	9.25	0	0	6/2
R.M. Hogg	6	12	0	95	36	7.92	0	0	0
J.D. Higgs	5	10	4	46	16	7.67	0	0	0
P.H. Carlson	2	4	0	23	21	5.75	0	0	2
G. Dymock	3	6	1	28	11	5.60	0	0	0
A.G. Hurst	6	12	2	44	17*	4.40	0	0	1
T.J. Laughlin	1	2	0	7	5	3.50	0	0	2
A.M. Hilditch	1	2	0	4	3	2.00	0	0	2

Australia Bowling

	I	O	M	R	W	Avge	5i	BB
R.M. Hogg	11	217.4	60	527	41	12.85	5	6/74
A.G. Hurst	11	204.2	44	577	25	23.08	1	5/28
J.D. Higgs	10	196.6	42	468	19	24.63	1	5/148
G. Dymock	6	114.1	19	269	7	38.43	0	3/38
P.H. Carlson	3	46	10	99	2	49.50	0	2/41
A.R. Border	3	31	13	50	1	50.00	0	1/31
B. Yardley	8	113.2	12	389	7	55.57	0	3/41
G.J. Cosier	3	12	3	35		—		
T.J. Laughlin	2	25	6	60	0	—		

England Batting and Fielding

	M	I	NO	R	HS	Avge	100	50	c/s
D.I. Gower	6	11	1	420	102	42.00	1	1	4
D.W. Randall	6	12	2	385	150	38.50	1	2	4
I.T. Botham	6	10	0	291	74	29.10	0	1	9
R.W. Taylor	6	10	2	208	97	26.00	0	1	18/2
G. Miller	6	10	0	234	64	23.40	0	1	1
G.A. Gooch	6	11	0	246	74	22.36	0	1	9

G. Boycott	6	12	0	263	77	21.92	0	1	4
J.M. Brearley	6	12	1	184	53	16.73	0	1	5
J.K. Lever	1	2	0	24	14	12.00	0	0	1
J.E. Emburey	4	7	1	67	42	11.17	0	0	6
R.G.D. Willis	6	10	2	88	24	11.00	0	0	3
M. Hendrick	5	9	4	34	10	6.80	0	0	4
P.H. Edmonds	1	1	0	1	1	1.00	0	0	1
C.M. Old	1	1	1	29	29*	—	0	0	0

England Bowling

	I	O	M	R	W	Avge	5i	BB
J.K. Lever	2	15.1	2	48	5	9.60	0	4/28
G. Miller	10	177.1	54	346	23	15.04	1	5/44
M. Hendrick	10	145	30	299	19	15.74	0	3/19
J.E. Emburey	8	144.4	49	306	16	19.13	0	4/46
C.M. Old	2	26.7	2	84	4	21.00	0	2/24
R.G.D. Willis	12	140.3	23	461	20	23.05	1	5/44
I.T. Botham	10	158.4	25	567	23	24.65	0	4/42
P.H. Edmonds	2	13	2	27	0	—		
G.A. Gooch	2	6	1	15	0	—		
G. Boycott	1	1	0	6	0	—		

TOUR AVERAGES (First-class matches only)

Batting and Fielding

	M	I	NO	R	HS	Avge	100	50	c/s
D.W. Randall	10	18	2	763	150	47.69	2	4	7
R.W. Tolchard	3	5	1	142	72	35.50	0	2	12
J.M. Brearley	11	21	5	538	116*	33.62	1	3	11
D.I. Gower	12	20	1	623	102	32.79	1	3	7
G. Boycott	12	23	3	533	90*	26.65	0	4	5
G. Miller	11	18	3	398	68*	26.53	0	2	5
I.T. Botham	9	14	0	361	74	25.79	0	3	14
G.A. Gooch	13	23	1	514	74	23.36	0	3	13
R.W. Taylor	10	15	2	230	97	17.69	0	1	36/6
P.H. Edmonds	7	9	2	115	38*	16.43	0	0	8
C.M. Old	6	6	1	81	40	16.20	0	0	2
C.T. Radley	6	9	0	138	60	15.33	0	1	2
R.G.D. Willis	10	13	4	115	24	12.78	0	0	3
J.E. Emburey	9	12	2	101	42	10.10	0	0	9
J.K. Lever	6	7	0	67	28	9.57	0	0	1
M. Hendrick	8	12	4	68	20	8.50	0	0	6

(D.L. Bairstow appeared in minor games only)

Bowling

	I	O	M	R	W	Avge	5i	BB
M. Hendrick	15	184.4	40	399	28	14.25	1	5/11
G. Miller	18	277.1	74	607	36	16.86	2	6/56
J.E. Emburey	16	261.1	73	563	31	18.16	1	5/67
I.T. Botham	16	239.3	44	848	44	19.27	1	5/51
R.G.D. Willis	19	210.3	34	696	34	20.47	1	5/44
C.M. Old	11	138	24	452	21	21.52	1	6/42
J.K. Lever	12	191.1	18	377	13	29.00	0	4/28
P.H. Edmonds	11	147	33	397	11	36.09	1	5/52
G.A. Gooch	10	26	2	80	1	80.00	0	1/16
G. Boycott	3	3	0	11	0	—		
D.W. Randall	1	2	0	9	0	—		
C.T. Radley	1	1	0	4	0	—		

Index